# Lord, I'm Listening

## Donna Leonard

This book is designed for your personal reading pleasure and profit. It is also designed for group study. A Leader's Guide with helps and hints for teachers is available from your local Christian bookstore or from the publisher at $2.25.

D0958081

## VICTOR BOOKS

a division of SP Publications, Inc., Wheaton, Illinois

Offices also in Fullerton, California • Whitby, Ontario, Canada • London, England

Recommended Dewey Decimal Classification: 248.3
Suggested subject heading: Devotional Literature

Library of Congress Catalog Card Number: 78-63637
ISBN: 0-88207-745-7

VICTOR BOOKS
A division of SP Publications, Inc.
P.O. Box 1825 • Wheaton, Illinois 60187

# Contents

*(handwritten annotations)*

1 Need
2 Motivation
3 Prep for
4 Training
5 Discernment in Listening
6 Applicat.
Insight

Discernment in Listening A How you know it
B How you study into God's Word

Devotions

. . . He entered a certain village;
and a woman named Martha welcomed Him into her home.

And she had a sister called Mary, who moreover was
                listening to the Lord's Word,
                  seated at His feet.

But Martha was distracted with all her preparations;
and she came up to Him, and said, "Lord, do You not care
that my sister has left me to do all the serving alone?
Then tell her to help me."

But the Lord answered and said to her, "Martha, Martha,
you are worried and bothered about so many things;
but only a few things are necessary,
                  really only one:
          for Mary has chosen the good part,
        which shall not be taken away from her."

                        —Luke 10:38-42

# Preface

Bombarded by books, seminars, and courses on varying degrees of total womanhood, men's opinions, and television, many Christian women fumble in the fog, wondering where the joy of the Christian life is and where their ministry lies. They are thoroughly frustrated, wondering if their God-given talents are to be hidden in a church kitchen or nursery forever. Some have been told they are out of God's will if they teach a Sunday School class of boys older than junior age. Others are informed that they should be allowed to be Directors of Christian Education, and still others are to be ordained and preach the Word! It has been pointed out that single women, who have gone to the mission field and taught God's Word to men and even won them to His Kingdom, should be expected to take their place in the "chain of command," under the leadership of a man, when they step onto home soil.

After listening to, discussing, and investigating men's opinions and translations concerning ministry for women in and out of the church, I have discovered that there are as many opinions as there are people giving them. We soon find ourselves listening to every source but God. No wonder we are frustrated!

It seems that listening to God's opinions has become a rare activity, even in Christian circles. It is my conclusion that God Himself will have to give me the answer for my life through His Word and the time I spend listening to Him. Only then will I know how to minister where He wants me.

Through the exciting experience of practicing God's presence in our lives we soon realize that He may have plans for us which we would have never imagined! A great variety of ministries is beginning to unfold for single and married women, but it takes a perceptive spiritual ear to know just where the Lord wants *you*.

When it comes to wanting to know how to listen to God, we become great book readers and seek earfuls of advice. Until we actually *listen* to Him, however, we can never experience the joy of His thoughts permeating ours. After devouring God's Word for His advice on listening, meditating, silence, stillness, and quietness, we can learn to live without all the input from the world. We can then become God-pleasers rather than men-pleasers.

Lord, I had asked You
          to teach me . . .
and then I'd gone my way.
          I had never listened.

I had sought Your advice,
          and then I'd leaned on my own . . .
          I had never listened.

I had yearned for Your presence,
          and had talked on and on . . .
          I had never listened.

Now, I stop,
          silent,
          waiting,
          listening.

Now Your voice
          softly,
          quietly
          speaks . . .
          as I listen.

# Our Need for Listening

1

The hotel shook as a bomb fell a few miles away. The Yom Kippur War had broken out during our second day in Cairo, Egypt, and for two weeks we could neither leave the city nor communicate with anyone outside it. We were stuck. We slept fitfully, in our clothes, never knowing when the air raid siren would sound. Fully aware that we would not reach our desired destination—Israel—we prayed, had Bible studies, took our turns with dysentery, and waited out the war.

For some other American tourists, however, it was a two-week nightmare. One tour leader abandoned his group. Another group disbanded, leaving each member to find his own way out. Though a ship from a Common Market nation enabled European tourists to flee, Americans were not allowed on the ship, so we were left behind. At night, from our seventh floor windows, we watched the lights from the distant Suez fighting. As we ate the meals the hotel provided, we were reminded of the verse, "Thou preparest a table before me in the presence of mine enemies" (Ps. 23:5, KJV).

One day as I walked down the hall of our hotel, I suddenly said aloud, "Lord, why am I not more worried? I should be frantic!" The Lord's presence was so real to me that He could have materialized and I wouldn't have been startled. It was as if He had answered immediately, "Because you are My child, and I am taking care of you." He made me so aware of His closeness that I wanted to stand in that special spot and not move.

Our miracle ship finally came into the war zone waters of Alexandria. It had been commandeered, half the crew had jumped ship, and it was too small for the several hundred Americans trying to escape. We would have to help serve tables; our rooms were incredibly tiny; we would have to share our "closet room" with another couple; but we couldn't have cared less. The Lord had answered our prayers—He had delivered us from Egypt!

When we returned home and I continued my quiet times, I noticed that the sense of the Lord's actual presence was not as distinct as it had been in Cairo. I asked Him, "Do I have to be in another war to know Your presence like that?" I longed for Him to be close to me. My quiet times had been quite sporadic—consistent when I needed Him, then inconsistent when things seemed to go along smoothly.

After a few weeks of this inner frustration, the turning point came. I began to think seriously of keeping a devotional notebook. My husband, Stan, had suggested this several years before and had begun one himself, but I could not take time for it. Since Stan and I had always been "sounding boards" for each other, it was frustrating to me when I desperately needed someone to talk to and he was not available. So with the thought, "Well, it wouldn't hurt to talk to the Lord," I began writing to Him. As I wrote, buried thoughts and feelings surfaced. I was able to verbalize as never before.

That was only the beginning. The notebook grew. I recalled the lessons learned while in Egypt during the Yom Kippur War. It made me realize that writing down my thoughts there had helped to:
- release tension
- verbalize thoughts not "taken out" on someone else. (Remember the advice about writing a letter and tearing it

up? We don't need to tear them up with the Lord—He accepts our feelings.)

• organize and sift through my feelings
• clarify and stabilize my relationship with the Lord
• establish peace instead of panic.

These five points were verified at home as my letters to the Lord increased. The growing took more and more time as I learned to know the Lord better. Second Peter 1:5 took on new meaning, ". . . You must learn to know God better and discover what He wants you to do" (LB). I soon realized that this hunger for the Lord, and new dimension in listening, could have occurred without my experiencing a war.

Not all of us have unusual circumstances that drive us to the Lord's side. He *wants* a dynamic relationship with us. He *longs* for us to listen to Him so we can be good models of Him (Isa. 30:18). He *commands* us to wait, to be silent before Him. You will discover some of these verses in the exercise at the end of the chapter. These commands alone should be motivation enough to want to please Him.

## Perspectives on Priorities

As my quiet times grew in length from 10 minutes, then to 20, and on to one hour (to my surprise!) situations occurred where I had to make a choice. Either I would have to put God in a box for five to ten minutes a day so that I could prepare for teaching and seminars, or I could drop some outside activities in order to enjoy God's presence and linger there. Wrestling with this decision wasn't easy because service for the Lord seemed so attractive (and still does), especially particular ministries that would have been exactly what I had been waiting for.

One day I suddenly remembered a conversation Stan and I had had on a Nile Hilton Hotel balcony. As we looked at the Giza pyramids and wondered how Joseph had felt when he had seen them, we thought about *time,* about our pursuit of education and ministry. We marveled at how the Lord had used Joseph in such a mighty way, even though he had been stuck in Egypt against his will. We talked about our years of walking with the Lord and what in our ministry would be the most fruitful for His eternal Kingdom if He should take us home to be with Him during that war? We evaluated the different phases of our lives and realized that only the people we had pointed to the Lord could be laid before Him as worthwhile. Our status, our knowledge, and popularity didn't count. Yet, at one time these had seemed so important—especially an advanced degree for our particular profession. But there in Egypt, miles from home, it just didn't seem to mean that much.

The Lord wasn't going to ask us if we had obtained a Ph.D. degree when we stood before Him. It seemed to us that our relationships with people were much more important. So much of what had seemed important to us at one time just melted away.

As the Lord paraded these thoughts before my memory, I thanked Him for reminding me of these perspectives. It was going to be a lot easier to say no to many activities now. Things that had been important before were not essential now. If the Lord led in certain directions, we would definitely follow, but not with the previous sense of urgency. Time with Him had precedence now, even at the expense of some outside activities. I longed to get to know Him better, to be like Him, to sense His presence daily, to listen constantly to what He wanted me to do, how He wanted me to live. And what joy there was in listening!

• • •

### Peace in War

Time stops for us and war begins
A place confined, with no way out—
                    just pray and wait.
    What good—popularity?
    What good—knowledge?
    What good—importance?

We stop and look at our life past.
Of things for You, what most shall last—
    Works, education, fame?
    No, none of that.

But people helped through hurt and pain
And pointed to our Saviour's way—
    *This* shall last!

As bombs fall down and buildings shake,
As fear looms near and friends forsake,
    at every turn an enemy—
    our every comment heard . . .
We would not be the least surprised
If You, dear Lord, materialized . . .
    so keenly is Your presence felt.

    Eternity a breath away . . .
    No regrets of yesterday . . .
      Your love enfolds us,
      Your strength upholds us,

    And we have peace.

        *—14 days in Cairo, Egypt*
        *Yom Kippur War*

● ● ●

## Bogged Down in Busyness

Early in our marriage Stan and I were caught in the whirlpool of *busyness* for the Lord, which left little or no time for real *listening* to Him. We threw ourselves into our ministry and before long were going too hard and too fast, unaware that this was the road many Christians take to emotional and mental illness.

We were like a ship which once anchored off a tropical

coast. In such a climate, where underwater growth is phe-nomenal, lily pads and their flowers soon grew to the bottom of the ship, making it their prisoner. The crew had a tre-mendous task of cutting apart this growth to free the ship.

Like this ship, many Christians are bound by "sanctified" schedules, deadlines, and time limits, to the point where stress can cause serious physical damage. It is a fact that heart attacks, once happening to men in their 40s and 50s, now occur among men in their early 30s. We can become so ex-cited about being used of the Lord that we forget about taking proper care of our bodies. We overbook ourselves until our emotional reserves are completely drained, and then wonder why we don't have the joy of the Lord in our lives. We get caught by the beautiful lily pads until we become immoveable. I have seen Christians become "busy, barren, and bitter" instead of "friendly, fruitful, and fragrant" simply because their philosophy was to "burn out" for the Lord. I maintain that the Lord gave us instructions on how to take care of our temples and He set for us a good example. He not only stated that we should "come away and rest awhile" (Mark 6:31), but He did it Himself. He often went off alone somewhere to have rest and fellowship with His Father before He ministered.

Overcommitting ourselves can be very dangerous. If we are willing servants in the church, we can expend ourselves and be dictated to until we are useless to anyone. We can easily become people-pleasers rather than God-pleasers. When we learn to say no, and spend that extra time with the Lord, He can tell us what *He* wants us to do, whether or not *He* wants us to take that extra speaking engagement or church responsibility. None of us is indispensable. One of the most difficult lessons I ever learned as a Christian was to get my priorities straight. Christ first, husband second, children third (in our case, spiritual children), then the ministry God has given. The Apostle Paul wrote to Timothy, "If anyone does not know how to manage his own family, how can he take care of God's church?" (3:5, NIV) This question referred to church leaders, but the pattern is clear for all in the church.

Family priorities and church life are not to be confused. God does not say one thing for the leaders and another for the followers.

One of my desires is to be a signpost that reflects Christ in such a way that people can look right past it to the Lord Himself. As teachers in a Christian college, my husband and I are always aware that students are very observant. If the model is Christlike and desirable, the student will begin to imitate it, but if the model is poor and inconsistent, the student becomes frustrated and turns it off. Jesus said, "A pupil is not above his teacher, but everyone, after he has been fully trained, will be like his teacher." (Luke 6:40). If we are to become models for others to follow, then we must take heed as to how our modeling affects them.

Later in this book we will discuss obedient life-style, and share ways the Lord has told us to minister, some of which may seem untraditional. I am content, knowing that I am fully responsible to my heavenly Father for my service to Him, and not to other people. When we listen to His directions for us, we cannot go wrong. We have never had such joy since listening to Him for His life-style for us.

• • •

### Dialogue on Busyness

My life has become too full, Lord
  with busy schedules and squeezed itineraries,
  filled-up calendars and booked-up days.
You must shake your head at us, Lord,
  as we run around, like ants
  scurrying, hurrying,
  rushing—to where?
But, then, Lord, we must use every minute!
  We can't be wasteful,
  It's because we love You so
  That we overwork!

> *Is it? Or is it to impress others?*
> *If you love Me,*
>   *you'll spend more time*
>     *becoming like Me,*
>   *and less time*
>     *being like others.*

But Lord, we want to be good examples for others—
"Modeling" it's called by some . . .

> *It's not the accelerated life*
>   *I want for you,*
>   *but the quiet life . . .*
> *I'm not impressed by "busyness,"*
>   *So why should you be?*
> *Busyness is not synonymous*
>   *With godliness.*

• • •

**Exercise** 1
Look up the following verses and fill in the accompanying blanks—write a sentence about what the verse says to *you*.

Waiting—What does God tell me?

Psalm 27:14 _____

Psalm 119:114 _____

Quietness

Isaiah 30:15b _____

1 Timothy 2:1-2 _____

1 Peter 3:3-4 _____

Silence

Habakkuk 2:20 _____

Zephaniah 1:7 _____

Psalm 62:1 _____

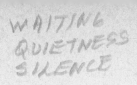

## Stillness

Psalm 46:10 _____

Psalm 4:4b _____

## Listening

Mark 4:23-24 _____

Hosea 14:9 _____

Matthew 13:9 _____

On the basis of these answers, what action will I take this week?

_____

Whom will I ask to check up on me? _____

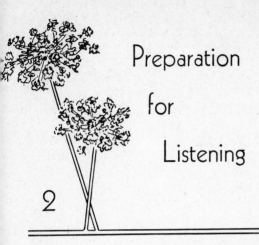

# Preparation for Listening

## 2

"Wow!!! . . . I love writing prayers to God—it helps me to be more honest, to let Him in on more details of my life. It is such a joy to look back and see growth and attitude changes in my life."

• • •

"I find it hard to spend only one hour alone with God each day. My prayers have become more specific for others and myself as I see answers written down on the opposite side of the page!"

• • •

"A problem that I have always had has been having a consistent and meaningful time with the Lord. Beginning a Quiet Time Notebook . . . has helped immensely! . . . It's been so great for me to visualize Christ sitting next to me; now He's really real to me."

• • •

"Listening to God . . . was the key for me and I discovered that by listening I got answers. I no longer had to be concerned with what everyone else thought but more with what was right for me. . . . The busy days when I took that precious time made them much more joyous than before. I shared the concept of the quiet time notebooks with my mother's Bible study group—women from 45—70. They loved it and I have seen growth in their lives due to it."

•   •   •

"How can you evaluate something that has changed your life to a much more meaningful and deep relationship with the Lord? The last 12 weeks I have grown in the Lord more than any other time in the 21 years I have lived, and the major reason has been using my notebook alongside God's Word."

•   •   •

"More than once when I faced disappointment and wanted to bathe myself in self-pity and despair, I turned to my notebook and wrote to God all that I felt, and He gave me His peace."

•   •   •

"The most exciting part of my notebook is where I write all prayer requests and their answers, because it gives written proof of what God is doing in my life. I get very excited when I reread this section."

•   •   •

"My Quiet Time Notebook has helped me to be more consistent and to put more organization and order into my quiet time and prayer life."

•   •   •

"I am more wholeheartedly dedicated to the idea of maintaining a Quiet Time Notebook than ever before. Both because of the realization through this past couple of months of the value and effect in the lives of all of us involved—regardless of the time it takes."

• • •

"Writing down the things I learned helped me to keep my mind from wandering and it also made a longer lasting impression on me. I'm glad that I have something to go back to and read too; it makes God's teaching really tangible."

• • •

. . . And on and on go the comments of people who have faithfully used a quiet time notebook as a spiritual tool for growth alongside God's Word. God puts the desire for such a notebook within the heart of many Christians, regardless of age, occupation, or ministry. Keeping a journal with the Lord has helped them cope with everyday life.

## How to Set up a Notebook

*Purchase a looseleaf notebook, lined paper, and tabs for divisions.* You may want a full 8½" x 11" size or a medium-sized notebook to carry with you at all times. Some people prefer the full-sized, large-ring notebook which allows for a great deal to be written.

*Create your own title—make it your very own special notebook.* Mine used to be called "Secrets with God," but since I was soon sharing my "refreshment pages," they were no longer secrets. Therefore I changed the title to "My Earthly Pilgrimage with God." Other titles which may trigger your imagination are, "Rooted and Built Up," "Beside Still Waters," or "Moments with My Messiah."

*Identify Tabs.* Your tabs will probably be different from those presented here. These are described only as guidelines for you to tailor your notebook to your needs.

## Tab Divisions

My husband Stan and I have a huge candle which we keep in the living room all year long. On New Year's Eve we light this candle and thank the Lord for what He has done for us the past year, enumerating all the blessings. Then we make new priorities for the coming year—measurable ones! (One year we decided to start saving for a trip to Israel—and if it weren't for the establishment of that priority, we would have never begun!)

*Priorities/Covenants. Priorities* can be for a week, for a semester, for a month, or for a year. It is rewarding to go back to them and with a red pen write a sentence or two about how each was met. When we are willing to sit down with the Lord and establish specific goals in our lives, it is amazing how much He can accomplish through us.

*Covenants* are rarely made at our house because we know God does not want us to make a vow unless we are willing to keep it. On the *Priorities/Covenants* tab page in my notebook, I have listed the following verses as a reminder to me that when I make a vow to the Lord, I know that He expects me to keep it.

Psalm 76:11a: "Make vows to the Lord your God and fulfill them."

Numbers 30:2: "If a man makes a vow to the Lord, or takes an oath to bind himself with a binding obligation, he shall not violate his word; he shall do according to all that proceeds out of his mouth."

Matthew 5:33: ". . . the ancients were told, 'You shall not make false vows, but shall fulfill your vows to the Lord.' "

Deuteronomy 23:21-23: "When you make a vow to the Lord your God, you shall not delay to pay it, for it would be sin in you, and the Lord your God will surely require it of you. However, if you refrain from vowing, it would not be sin in you. You shall be careful to perform what goes out from your lips, just as you have voluntarily vowed to the Lord your God, what you have promised."

This very book is the result of a pact made with the Lord. It began during a women's retreat at Arrowhead Springs, California. After my talk about listening to the Lord, many of the women confirmed with me that this had been their own secret of coping with stress and the pace of life. Some asked for the material in written form and said they knew others who were hungry for the Lord but didn't know how to go about learning to know Him better.

After I returned home, the Lord and I had a long discussion about it. For several days, the thought of writing down the material on listening to the Lord overwhelmed me. I argued that everything I wanted to say had already been said by others, in different ways, perhaps, but it was there somewhere. Yet He impressed on my mind the need for such material, especially for people who were caught up with so many pressures and had never learned to really listen to Him.

Finally I told the Lord, "If you really want me to undertake this job, I am willing. But please give me some sign that it is from You and not my own imagination." I wrote a covenant on October 5, saying that each morning I would work on the project for a few hours, but that He in some way was to give me a sign that it was from Him. He gave me a distinct impression that I was not to talk about this to anyone, not even Stan (which was extremely difficult, since one week later he suggested that I write something for a "Roles of Women" course!). I even went so far as to promise the Lord that I would not reveal to anyone what was going on until He impressed on my mind that it could be revealed.

Even after beginning the project, I felt insecure and continued to ask the Lord if He was sure He knew what He was doing! My daily devotions were in the Book of Exodus and the stories of Moses, and every time Moses said, "Not me, Lord," I echoed those same words. I had no idea how the Lord was going to encourage me, but I kept reminding Him of my fleece. Each morning the work continued, little by little.

On October 7, I had a dream—hang on! Because of frightening nightmares in the past, I have established a habit of verbally committing my subconscious mind to the Lord as I crawl into bed for the night. Though this has been a marvelous cure and a real help for peaceful sleep, it has never made me a believer in modern-day visions or dreams. But this one astounded me. In the dream the Lord, Stan, and I were sitting together. The Lord nodded—nothing was said. Then we nodded in agreement as a large "26" superimposed itself on all three of us. The people faded, but the number stayed. The next morning, I wrote in my notebook that maybe it was the date in October that He wanted me to tell Stan. I felt peace about it, although I didn't understand it at all. Known to no one but the Lord and me, work kept progressing.

A few weeks later, Stan came home from Biola College, where we teach, with the announcement, "Guess what! The 'Leadership Roles of Men' class was approved today to be taught next semester." The statement took my breath away— the date was October 26!—and I had not even been aware that this course was going to be presented for approval! I felt cleared to tell Stan about the project. It was as if the Lord was saying, "OK, now you can tell him." I also understood the whole dream. The book I was working on was to be originally for a "Leadership Roles of Women" class, but the Lord had wanted me to wait until confirmation of the men's class. This was the sign that it was from Him, not me.

The covenant had been kept! I went back to that page and tearfully wrote in bright red letters, "Covenant kept! Praise the Lord!"

*Refreshment Pages.* These pages will form the next section of your notebook. You may include favorite songs, poems, or prose which God gives to you or others—anything that helps you draw closer to God. Sometimes when you sit down for your quiet time and feel extra dry, quietly singing some of the songs or reading some of the prose can help you to feel Him next to you. One of my favorite pages is a newsletter written by our pastor. Its title is "Quietness" and it's refreshing to read it over from time to time.

*Bible Studies.* Your favorite kind of Bible study can be placed in this section. Maybe you prefer inductive, trace-a-topic, or a word study. Most people like to separate their Bible study from their quiet time. A quiet time is different from a Bible study in that your personal time with the Lord should be a listening-talking process, a two-way conversation with Him. Study can bind communication, and when this happens, actual fellowship with the Lord becomes nonexistent.

Once in a while in this horrendous pace of life you will have one or two days during the week where you have some extra time. Then your quiet time and Bible study can be combined. Your study can become extra rich with meaning when you commune with Him about the new truths He has just taught you. Priority time means quality time with your Saviour, when you don't feel pressured, and when you can linger with Him and talk to Him casually.

*Letters to God*. "What?!!" my friend gasped in horror. "You actually write down your feelings—*everything?* What if the Lord came, and someone found the letters and read them?"

"If it would bring him to the Lord, great!" was my answer. I believe that after the church has been caught up from the earth, some of the unsaved may not only find the Lord through His Word, but also through some of these notebooks. So I do not feel the least bit inhibited by telling the Lord exactly how I feel. When I am open and honest with Him, He then comes to me with the most comfort, making His presence more real to me than ever before.

A format often helps in writing these letters. This one has worked well for many people:

In the upper left-hand corner write the verse that "stood out" to you as you read the Scripture that morning. Sometimes there will be two or three verses, or no verse at all. If you want to memorize the verse, copy it on a separate card. The date in the top right corner and reference of the entire passage read will help you know where you are reading each day (sometimes from two different passages). If you miss a day, the date tells you so. If you do miss a day, however, do not go on a guilt trip because of it. As I've developed my notebook, I've lost the "duty" feeling of having my quiet times. Now it is an "I can't wait!" feeling to be with my Lord. I asked the Lord to teach me and He took me at my word! Making me hunger for Him more and more is part of the lesson I am learning.

If you feel prompted to pray for someone after you've

written several lines of your letter to God, stop, pray, then go on. Where I stop I usually draw some asterisks to remind me that at that time there was some precious communication with the Lord. Sometimes the asterisks may represent a poem or a bit of prose. Then I keep right on writing to the Lord. You may want to write down what the passage meant to you, or you may want to ventilate a difficult situation that occurred that day or several days before.

On some days your letters will be epistles, page after page. On other days, you may get so caught up in the quiet worship of enjoying His presence that only a few lines will be sufficient. During these times it may seem that the Lord is using your fingers to write some of the most glorious prose you can imagine. It is because He is right there with you, wanting you to experience the joy of His presence.

*Prayer Requests.* Short-range and long-range requests should be kept on separate pages in your notebook. All my requests used to be in one section, and soon the request pages became longer and longer. I was committed to praying for all these people, but there are only so many hours in a day. I was in a predicament! What was I going to do?

One of my friends had asked me to pray for God's will regarding a husband for her. Could I expect a prayer like this to be answered in the next day or so? Of course not. Common sense indicated that my long list should be divided into short-range and long-range requests. This idea worked for me; it may also work for you. To better remember each request, divide up the requests by the days of the week. For example, Monday could be the day to pray for your family requests. Tuesday might be for requests concerning close friends' short-range requests. Wednesday could be a day for requests relating to your ministry. Thursday may be "special problems" day— praying for people you know who are in broken home situations, who have lost their jobs, who are in especially difficult circumstances. Friday could be long-range request day. Saturday could be discipleship needs, for those to whom you have witnessed or whom you want to come to the Lord. Saturday at our house is the day for our "spiritual children"—students at Biola who have hurts and have asked for prayer.

Dividing the requests in this way insures prayer and helps prevent the "duty" feeling. But this doesn't mean that the requests are remembered only on certain days. Often when I see a student at school, or drive by a student's off-campus apartment, I whisper a prayer for him. When a letter comes in the mail from home, the Lord urges me to pray for that situation right then. As I work in the garden or do the dishes I can also think about and pray for people. It also helps my thought life to be more pure. Instead of pitying myself in a certain situation, praising God and praying for others has been a most rewarding and healthy stimulation for me.

When Stan and I began jogging around the college track, we established a habit of praying for a different person in our family on each lap around the track. Not only did the jogging time go faster, but we felt good, having had fellowship with the Lord as He went right around the track with us!

One of the greatest thrills is discovering how the Lord answers prayer requests. As you can see below, a relatively large space is left for the "Date Answered" column. This space is for little notes you may make from week to week, indicating that you are to wait, or that the situation in question is improved, but not completely answered. Then when the answer does come, write a big PTL! (Praise the Lord!) and how your prayer was answered. Checking up on people as you pray for them is a big encouragement to them too. The development of your caring ministry can be one of the most

| Date | Request | Date Answered & How |
|------|---------|---------------------|
|      |         |                     |

exciting things that has ever happened to you. James encouraged Christians to pray for one another (James 5:16), and keeping track of answers to those prayers is a real blessing.

*Schedule or Calendar.* You will soon discover that as you sit down to spend some time with the Lord, distractions will loom before you. You will remember that you want to call "so-and-so," that you should write a letter to your sister, that your houseplants haven't been watered for a week and a half. This is the time to ask for the Lord's help. You might take a sheet of paper from the back of your notebook and write down all the things that need your attention. Then say something like, "OK, Lord, these are all the things I need to do today. Since they are preventing me from just enjoying You, I ask for Your wisdom about which need top priority and which can wait until last." Then sit in silence a few minutes. Open your eyes, look at the list, and try to use your God-given common sense. Having asked for His wisdom, number the items on the list in order of their priority. Then lay the list aside, and begin your time with Him. When He helps you with the lists, you will find that more has been accomplished by the end of the day and you probably won't get so irritated if everything didn't get done. He will help you see your responsibilities from His perspective.

Some people have even kept calendars in this section of their notebooks and a month or so at a time have jotted down appointments or people they must remember to call.

## Exercise
(Check off steps as you complete them.)

*Step 1:* Purchase a looseleaf notebook, paper, tabs.

*Step 2:* Identify tabs of the divisions you want to have in your notebook.

*Step 3:* List prayer requests and divide them by days of the week. (See next page worksheet.)

*Step 4:* Begin a short-range request page with dates as seen in format on page 29.

*Step 5:* Begin a long-range request page with dates as seen in format on page 29.

Place both of these request pages behind your division of prayer requests.

## Worksheet

List prayer requests below:

| | |
|---|---|
| 1. | 8. |
| 2. | 9. |
| 3. | 10. |
| 4. | 11. |
| 5. | 12. |
| 6. | 13. |
| 7. | 14. |

Divide the requests by the days of the week.

| Monday: | Thursday: |
|---|---|
| 1. | 1. |
| 2. | 2. |
| 3. | 3. |
| Tuesday: | Friday: |
| 1. | 1. |
| 2. | 2. |
| 3. | 3. |
| Wednesday: | Saturday: |
| 1. | 1. |
| 2. | 2. |
| 3. | 3. |

Put this in your Quiet Time Notebook, just behind your prayer requests tab.

# Our Motivation
# for
# Listening

3

"How do I wait on God—listen to Him?"

"How do I really pray?"

"How do I combat the plateaus?"

"My quiet times never last more than five minutes and I don't feel like I'm growing. What can I do about it?"

"What *do* I do during my quiet time? Sure, I read a passage, then pray, but it seems like a duty."

"How do I keep from falling asleep? How can I really concentrate on what I am doing?"

Such questions as these are asked over and again by people who long for a dynamic relationship with the Lord. Since the very core of a joyous Christian life is our quiet time with God, let's look at some valid techniques of listening to Him.

## Prerequisites for Listening

*Same place, same hour, as much as possible.* There will be days when our schedules are upset or loved ones are visiting us and our "special time" is gone before we know it. The main thing is to not get so discouraged that if you miss a day, you quit altogether. Later in the day it might be possible to talk with the Lord when you can get alone with Him.

For many people, early morning seems best, before outside impressions have a chance to clutter the blotters of our mind. The Psalmist said, "In the morning, O Lord, Thou wilt hear my voice; in the morning I will order my prayer to Thee and eagerly watch" (Ps. 5:3).

You may be a night person, however, and feel more awake and aware at 10 P.M. than at 10 A.M. Meet with the Lord then. He doesn't hang out appointment schedules—He'll be there with you. Jesus found a place to pray alone in the evenings. "He went up to the mountain by Himself to pray; and when it was evening, He was there alone" (Matt. 14:23). He also had prayer times in the early morning (Mark 1:35).

Whether you have your quiet time in the morning or evening is not as important as the fact that you *do* establish a regular time to be with Him. One college student has an irregular schedule but meets with the Lord on a *regular* basis. She has early classes on Tuesdays and Thursdays, so has her quiet time in the afternoons on those days. On Mondays, Wednesdays, and Fridays, she meets with the Lord in the early morning.

*A quiet place, unhindered, unhurried.* "Impossible!" you say. Wait a minute! Before losing you altogether, let's look at some possibilities. They may not be ideal, but the Lord does not have prerequisites as to where He wants to meet with us. We choose the time and place, and He will be there. That is the beauty of it.

One woman has her quiet time while her small children have their afternoon naps. Another mother with young children asked her husband to stay with the children while she spent an hour in the public library conversing with the Lord. Several people we know, all in different life-styles, have had to resort to the privacy of their bathrooms to be uninterrupted —such is the congestion of our 20th century.

You may find it difficult to find a place by yourself, but remember that the Lord does not require ideal conditions— you demand that. If you have to, make a little sign and hang it on your door, "Thank you for not disturbing." Don't make it hard on yourself by insisting that everyone be out of your apartment or house. This often is unrealistic, and the Lord will meet with you even when others are around.

If you can find a spot where you can go regularly and where on some days you can spend longer times than on others, this will be a key to your success of listening to the Lord.

*Determination.* Don't let distractions stop you. They will *always* be there!

A loveseat in our bedroom at the back of our home is my sanctuary. Every morning on my way to this spot, I see a multitude of things I haven't quite caught up with or that really should be done. One thing that helps me resist these distractions is visualizing the Lord on the loveseat, waiting for me to come. Then if I stop to do something else on the way to my quiet time, I can almost hear the Lord saying, "Donna, I'm waiting for you. I'm here waiting to be with you." That speeds me on. If we are determined to give God top priority for the day, the reward of His presence is incomparable.

• • •

## To You First, I Go

To You first, I go, Lord . . . to search *Your* knowledge,
        then to my book to be read.
To You first, I go, Lord . . . to gain *Your* strength,
        then to my housework and chores.
To You first, I go Lord . . . to ask *Your* wisdom,
        then to my grading and letters.
To You first, I go, Lord . . . to seek *Your* attitudes and
        opinions, then to face the world's input.
To You first, I go, Lord . . . for *Your* gentleness and peace,
        then to my gardening and plants.
As I make my way to my secret place
        of quietness with You,
I almost need to close my eyes
        from distractions old and new.

They scream at me,
They reach at me,
To cheat me from Your best.
I breathe a prayer to get me there
to You, where I can rest.

• • •

Do you have trouble waking up in the morning? Some of the following courses of action may help.

• Get up earlier (if extra early hours are not your thing, washing your face with a hot washcloth helps).

• Put the alarm clock across the room.

• Take a shower and dress.

• Eat first if an empty stomach upsets you.

• Take a short walk or light jog around several blocks—this can be especially helpful if you have someone to go with you.

Early morning is a great time to talk with the Lord while you are exercising. Traffic is usually light at this time of day and people are still sleeping. Whoever goes with you can jog far enough ahead of you so that you can experience "aloneness" with the Lord. Not everyone can get out and run, however, so a quick shower or a drink of orange juice can do the trick of waking you up.

## Steps for Listening

Now to the most exciting part of all. You go to your special place to be with the Lord, to converse with Him and listen to Him. After you are there, then what? Just *how* do you listen to the Lord?

These steps [1] are merely a guide for you to follow. They do not need to be done in this order (except for the first one), and you will find that from day to day, you will be changing them around (or leaving some out) to suit your needs best.

*Sit silently before the Lord.* The Psalmist said, "My soul waits in silence for God only" (Ps. 62:1). As you wait before God, quietly ask Him if there is an attitude which needs to be confessed. Then wait for a few moments. You may want to read aloud Psalm 139:23-24 to the Lord: "Search me, O God, and know my heart. Try me and know my anxious thoughts. And see if there be any hurtful way in me, and lead me in the everlasting way." If the Lord has brought to your mind an attitude of unforgiveness toward someone, confess it. If He wants you to express love to that person in some way, write this down in your notebook so you will not forget it.

Psalm 66:18 indicates that if we have sin in our hearts, the Lord will not hear us, so confession is a very important step. If we try to converse with the Lord while sin is present in our lives, we are wasting our time. The joy of His presence can be felt only when our lives are clean channels for Him to use. If the Lord brings nothing to your mind—don't pass over this step too quickly; let the Holy Spirit do His work—you are ready for the next step.

*Begin praising and thanking God.* Doing this aloud will help keep you from daydreaming, going to sleep, or being distracted. As you talk, picture the Lord right next to you. If you are really hurting, picture His arms around you, holding you in comfort. Picture the Lord giving you His full attention. Concentrate on what the Lord might look like sitting visibly next to you as you sing quietly a song of worship. (Go to your refreshment section and use one of those songs.) The song, "There's a Sweet, Sweet Spirit in This Place," sung with singular pronouns rather than plural ones, seems to always make the Lord's presence felt. Do this with as many of the songs as possible. You can "whisper-sing" quietly, even with someone in the next room.

Some things to thank and praise Him for are:
His love for you,
the home He has given you,
freedom to worship and read His Word,
the heavenly home He is preparing for you,
His readiness to always be available to you,
your health—this could be taken from you at any time,
His answers to specific prayer.

*Ask the Lord to penetrate and guide your thoughts as you read His Word, and to make His presence felt to you as you read.*

Read the passage you have selected; then jot the reference and that day's date down in the top right corner of your notebook. If you are reading a portion that does not lend itself to spiritual refreshment (such as genealogies or numbering of the people), you might also want to read in the New Testament epistles or in the Psalms. It is important that you have some real spiritual meat to chew on for that day.

*Write your feelings in a letter to God.* Is there anything in the passage that speaks to you? Is there one verse that "pops out" from all the others? Write it in the top left corner. On some days, it will seem as if God is impressing on your mind certain attitudes and opinions. He will permeate your mind if you let Him.

Write down your feelings—how rotten you feel or how happy you are. Tell Him all the nitty-gritty about a certain situation. He wants you to know He is concerned for you and accepts all these feelings. Perhaps here the Lord will reveal to you that He wants *His* attitudes to be shown through your life. He might even show you that you need to confess some wrong before you can go further. Confess it and write down your confession. Writing it out even makes it more real. It makes His presence more keenly felt, because you are making a transaction with the Lord rather than saying a quick "I'm sorry" until the situation arises again. You'll remember then that you wrote down that confession in the presence of God, and it will take on a much deeper meaning.

During these times of writing and talking with the Lord He may bring to mind someone who needs encouragement. Ask the Lord specifically, "Lord, is there someone who especially needs a lift today? How can I help him—a note, cup of coffee, fresh flowers from our garden?" Many times He has deeply impressed someone on my mind, though not necessarily at the moment of request.

One particular morning, almost five hours after my quiet

time was over, He impressed on my mind one of my students who needed encouragement. At that moment I happened to be listening to a guest speaker at a prayer breakfast in the school cafeteria. For some reason, I felt an urge to look at the back of the room. There stood that student, his face crestfallen—the only person there who was obviously very unhappy. Right then the Lord seemed to say, "Write him a note." Inwardly, I asked the Lord, "But what should I say? I haven't the slightest idea what is bothering him!"

As soon as I got home from that meeting, I wrote the student a note of encouragement. The Lord seemed to impress on my mind words of affirmation, letting the student know we were praying for him. I had no idea what was troubling him, but I didn't need to—the Lord knew.

Later that day, this student stood at our front door. His first words after entering were, "Who told you? How did you know I was hurting? I had not told one person about my problem!"

I said, "God told me." I was as amazed as he was at the way God had worked!

God uses us when we listen. He makes us sensitive to others when we have first spent time with Him and learned of His sensitivity.

*Pray for items on your prayer list.* As you go to this section of your notebook and record how prayers are answered, you will feel a new excitement as you realize that God is real in your life. Your prayer list will not be cumbersome if you remember to divide the list by the days of the week, as suggested in chapter 2.

It is in praying for others that the joy of interceding is found. God answers in beautiful, sometimes unexpected, ways. You can know the thrill of watching His perfect timing. Remember to pray for *God's will* in every situation, not for your own.

*Learn from memory a verse of Scripture.* If you have problems memorizing, take heart. I am the type of person whose mind can go absolutely blank when I stand to quote a favorite verse in a sharing service. After several such embarrassing situations, I wanted to give up. I learned that about seven years of our lives are spent in waiting [2] however, and I was spurred on to a new endeavor to store away Scripture in my heart during these moments.

Let me share with you several ways to remember Scripture. After memorizing one or two short verses and saying them over to myself in my quiet time, I discovered that the calm they created within me helped me be more patient with others. So I tried a few more. Cutting up several 3″ x 5″ cards to fit a clear acetate holder purchased at a stationer's store, I discovered that a little packet of verses could go with me anywhere without bulk or weight—what a light treasure!

A special way to help me remember a verse is to take it from the version or paraphrase that is most meaningful to me. Then I print out the verse on the small card in such a way that my mind can visualize it as a picture. For example, instead of copying Philippians 4:8 in the usual line-by-line way, write it this way:

Phil. 4:8 (KJV)
Whatsoever things are true,
honest,
just,
pure,
lovely,
good report;
if there be any virtue and
if there be any praise,
THINK ON THESE THINGS.

The final instruction, *think on these things,* consists of *four* words. The items listed before the final instruction consist of *eight.* This helped me to remember the address of the verse: Philippians 4:8.

You might also print the verse so that a picture comes to your mind:

Psalm 73:25-26 (LB)
Whom have I in heaven but You?
And I desire no one on earth
as much as You!
My health fails
my spirts droop
YET GOD REMAINS!
He is the strength of my heart,
He is mine forever.

Now, instead of counting the cars of a train going by, I see how many verses I can remember. They come to mind while I'm doing dishes, feeling discouraged after a rough day, or when I'm tempted to criticize or grumble. The Lord has a wonderful way of bringing to mind the right verse just when I need it.

Before we leave this section, it is important to stress again that these steps need not be done in the same order each day, nor does every step need to be included every day! When you are consciously aware of God's presence and know that your heart is right with Him, it is a joy to begin a quiet time with a song or a letter to Him. Actual intercession after a short period of thanksgiving may be more natural on some days than on others.

One thing is certain—your quiet time will stay alive and vital. Ruth Rietveld, mother of two and a Christian home-maker, listens to sacred music when she wakes up with the blahs—this helps set her heart attitude for a spirit of worship with the Lord. Sometimes she listens to the *Living New Testament* on tape to soak up the atmosphere of a passage of Scripture. Though not considering herself a musical whiz, she often writes a contemporary poem based on a psalm she has just read, then puts a tune to it. She doesn't perform in public, but does it for her own enjoyment and heart-praise to the Lord. She feels that a good "visiting relationship" with Him is more important than keeping a rigid schedule of "so many chapters a day."

## Benefits of Listening

As you discover the Lord's presence with you in your quiet times, the *duty* feeling soon becomes an *I can't wait!* feeling. Some definite benefits can come because of spending this time daily with the Lord.

*It strengthens your self-identity and self-image.* Some of us have problems with a low self-image and feelings of little worth. As you get to know the Lord better and picture Him next to you, you will feel Him accepting everything you say. He doesn't put you down; He teaches you His attitudes. You leave your special place feeling more worthy than you did before you sat down next to Him.

*He helps you in your Christlikeness and daily growth* (2 Peter 1:5b-8, LB). As the Lord's attitudes and opinions flood your mind, *only then* can you begin to manifest the fruit of the Holy Spirit (Gal. 5:22-23) throughout the day. The more time you spend with Him, the more you become like Him. Often, as I begin reading a passage in the Gospels, I have asked Him to pluck me from this 20th century and plop me down into the first century A.D. so that I can see from His perspective what He wants me to learn. The passage takes on a whole new dimension as I picture the scene going on and "hear" Him say, "Now, today, this is how you can be like Me."

*He gives you His creative ideas and wisdom.* Often the Lord can plant creative ideas in your mind during these quiet times because you are still enough to listen to Him. As you ask for wisdom (James 1:5), the perception and discernment He will give you will simply amaze you. Many new ideas about your life-style may surface during this time. He will put gems of wisdom into your thoughts that you know very well are not yours but His.

*He keeps you cleansed for effective ministry.* The daily cleaning of the channels is proof positive that the Lord can use you. When you ask the Lord to cleanse you from bitter attitudes, resentments, and hurts, and then *take action to manifest your love* in some way to the person who has wronged you, the thrill of being used by Him is great.

Actually writing down these kinds of things has helped me tremendously. I used to just sit and inwardly take note of what I had done wrong, whisper a prayer of repentance, then go on my merry way until I found myself doing the same thing again. Now it is a much more serious step, since with the Lord by my side, I have a witness to my writing. He reminds me during the day to do as He would do in actions and attitudes toward others.

*It is healthful to the body as well as to the mind.* A quiet time brings tremendous physical benefits. Medical research has shown that meditation of some type or a period of daily quietness slows the heart rate and lowers blood pressure. Your regular quiet times can lower stress and in turn decrease the danger of hypertension and heart attacks. I'm aware that without these refreshments with the Lord, my body could be easily dissipated by 20th century pressure. Then it would simply be a matter of time before my destination would be a hospital bed.

## Listening on the Plateau

Webster says a plateau is "an *elevated* tract of level land." When we travel across the great mesas of the West, our car engine grinds as we climb, but soon the ground levels off and we are high on a flat place. The sunshine is brighter, and the air clearer, pollution no longer clogging our vision. We see things with a much better outlook. The fact that we are no longer climbing, however, doesn't mean we will always be here. Since we are elevated, we will either need to go back down, or climb even higher to mountain altitudes.

One of the biggest problems in my quiet times used to be the plateaus—when there seemed to be no growth at all. Remembering well-meaning pastors who had drummed into me, "If you are not growing, you are stagnant!" I felt guilty, wondering how to get out of the rut and back into the "growing" path. I pled with the Lord to reveal areas where I needed to forgive. One day it dawned on me that growth could *still* be taking place during the plateau periods of my life. The psalmist compared the righteous man to a "tree firmly planted by streams of water, which yields its fruit in its season" (Ps. 1:3, NASB); apparently we must have our seasons of growing. Even though our outward spurts of growth may seem to be at intervals, our inward maturing can be constant.

Houseplant owners are instructed not to overfeed or overwater their plants but to nourish them at certain intervals, so that when the period does come for the plants to bloom, they will flourish with glorious blossoms. If plant food is given continuously, we soon discover that the plants become "tired," discolored, or droopy. When our nurseryman instructed us to fertilize a new tree at certain times of the year, we listened. Continual fertilization can send all nourishment to the foliage and cheat the tree of choice fruit. The tree may seem dormant, but its roots are always taking nourishment. Even evergreens are to be pruned at a certain time of the year for better shape and beauty. These plant facts have encouraged me when my fruit seems to be scant. We can still be consciously aware of an around-the-clock listening to God, even on plateau days.

Sometimes our devotions may be so rich with meaning and so full of contentment with what the Lord is teaching that we feel like saying, "Enough, Lord, for now, I just can't take any more in!" Then we need times to chew the spiritual food He has given us, to swallow and digest it, to literally put these new lessons into practice in our relationships with others. The proof of our growth is in our actions, not in our closed-door closet with the Lord. We can be perfectly willing to learn, but will fail again and again until we respond to others in the spirit that Jesus would, regardless of our culture or century. Then we can thrill at new growth in our lives.

Now when plateaus occur, I no longer feel the need to fuss and worry. If the Lord has exposed nothing that needs to be confessed, I rest in Him and enjoy Him *by faith,* even though I may not *feel* His presence at those times.

The most important thing to remember during plateau days is that you can still feed on God's Word daily, and your roots can still grow, even if your "outward" appearance may be temporarily barren of leaves or fruit. Having quiet times is a matter of special discipline when you don't *feel* you are bearing fruit. If you confess sin as the Lord reveals it, if you give Him priority in regular quiet times with Him, He will bring you off the plateau in His time. The main thing is not to go on a guilt trip because of it. We all have dormant times, just as we all have fruit-bearing times.

This verse has been especially helpful to me during plateau days:

> WAIT for the Lord
> BE STRONG
> and let your heart take courage;
> yes,
> WAIT for the Lord.
> (Ps. 27:14)

Since it is so short, I can say it often to remind myself that perhaps the Lord wants me to see things from a new perspective—from the plateau view. This assures me that since I am in His will, He will inject me with new growth in His own timing.

• • •

### Pilgrimage by Faith

For Your presence in my quiet time,
    I thank You.
The feeling of You near is precious,
    and I am awed to absolute silence and worship.
For the times when You don't feel near,
    I thank You.
I accept by faith You are with me,
    and continue my journey.
For plateau days, times of resting
    I thank You.
For even through these, there are lessons for me,
    and I accept them with a teachable heart.

For this precious earthly pilgrimage with You
  I am thankful.
And that for minute to minute,
  from hour to hour,
This daily communication, sometimes joyously active,
          sometimes comfortably silent,
  is just a foundation for our friendship
          throughout eternity.

●  ●  ●

## Exercise

1. As you listen to the Lord in silence, audibly ask Him some of these questions:

a. Is there someone I need to forgive or something I need to confess?

b. Holy Spirit, have I grieved You in any way? (Wait, concentrate on Him. If the Lord reveals nothing to you, then ask:)

c. How do You want me to look at this particular situation that is bothering me—from Your viewpoint, Lord? (Write it down in a letter to Him.)

d. What fruit of the Spirit (Gal. 5:22-23) do You want me to especially manifest today?

e. What one quality of You can I reflect most today?

f. Is there someone who especially needs encouragement today?

g. How can I lift his or her spirit? By a phone call?
          A note?
          Flowers or plant?
          Coke or a cup of coffee?

2. If you have not written a letter to the Lord yet, do it now.

(Put page 45 in your quiet time notebook so that you can add questions that will help you.)

---

[1] The first, second, and fifth steps are adapted from chapters 9 and 10 of *What Happens When Women Pray* (Victor Books, 1973) by Evelyn Christenson.

[a] Carole Mayhall, *From the Heart of a Woman* (Colorado Springs, Colo.: NavPress) p. 27.

# Our Insights
# from
# Listening

4

Stephanie Radcliffe's world capsized one week. On Wednesday, her dishwasher broke. Then the fan belt on their car snapped so she and her husband had to borrow a truck to pick up unexpected company. On Thursday, the oven door broke, and her two children bought a pup. On Friday, Stephanie developed severe pains and had to make an emergency trip to the hospital. On Saturday, someone pushed the lawnmower over the sprinkler valve and sent a gusher into the air.

After reading Psalm 139 on Friday morning, Stephanie decided that she was powerless to keep her days from overturning. She was going to see how God would work things out. When Stan and I saw her a week later, her spirit was radiant. She had turned disaster into an adventure with God.

Because of Christ's presence in our quiet times, He can help each one of us develop a set of keys to joyous Christian living. The keys given in this chapter are merely a guide for you to follow—they have helped me most in my pilgrimage. You will need to develop a set of your own keys that will unlock doors of spiritual success for you. When something you have tried has helped you know the Lord better, make it a part of your daily living. This will be a secret to becoming the person God wants you to be.

The keys in this chapter have been developed over a period of time, after trial and error, and a bit of frustration. If you begin working on one key *now*, you can go at your own pace and add keys later on. As you consider keys for your daily victories, you might ask yourself these questions:

Is it healing? In what way?

Is it strengthening? How?

Can I know God's presence better in my life because of it?

What Christlike quality will it develop in me?

## KEY 1: An unhurried, unhindered quiet time with the Lord develops self-discipline (James 4:8a)

This key is *basic*. If your schedule prevents you from having such a time every day of the week, then plan for at least five days when you can just linger in the Lord's presence.

Within the structure of this key are several points to consider (also mentioned in chapter 3):

daily confession to the Lord;

daily cleansing by the Lord;

daily conversing with the Lord;

daily listening to the Lord;

development of a life pilgrimage notebook (Writing down your keys in your notebook would help establish the fact that you are working on them. Under each key, write your frustrations and progress. The Lord wants to help you with this); and

digging gems of spiritual truth.

Recently my husband and I enjoyed some amateur gold panning. A friend took us to a spot on the Yuba River back in the mother-lode country, where over a century ago gold miners sought their fortunes. With much patience we began the long, tedious task of gold panning. We scooped up sand and rocks from the river bottom into the sifting pan, and did our best to slosh the water around in just the "right" method, so that the excess sand could be washed off. Finally, after most of the sand and rocks were gone, black sand lay in a thin line at the pan bottom.

If a gold panner is fortunate, specks of gold dust will sparkle in that bit of leftover black sand. To prove the sparkles are real gold, they must be poured into a small bottle of water. If the gold specks sink immediately to the bottom of the bottle, they are gold dust. If they float slowly to the bottom, they are most likely pyrite, or "fool's gold." Gold panning is a time-consuming and patience-testing job—but what a thrill to find some gold dust, if one is willing to work for it!

Like panning for gold, discovering gems of spiritual truth in our quiet time does not always come easily. If we hurriedly sit down, speed-read a chapter, and mumble a prayer to the Lord, it is no wonder that we feel dry in our spiritual lives. When we ask the Holy Spirit to teach us from His Word, He will be faithful to make the words part of our thoughts, not just print on a page.

## KEY 2: Scripture memorization develops purity (Ps. 119:1; Phil. 4:8)

No one can tell you how much Scripture to memorize. The point is that you need not get discouraged if someone else seems to have a gift for memorization while you plod along, wondering if it is worth working on this key. It is worth it for me; Scripture memorization has been most instrumental in helping me maintain a positive attitude toward people and situations.

## KEY 3: Praise develops a rejoicing spirit (Ps. 119:164)

This key verse comes to my mind often and is quite easy to memorize: "I will praise You seven times a day because of Your wonderful laws" (LB). The Lord has often lifted my spirits during times of discouragement, just by bringing that verse to my mind. My husband and I have found that because we praise the Lord often, even when things aren't going so well, our home is a happy one.

One of our former students was in our home several weeks ago and reminded us of how we had exhorted her to praise the Lord, and thank Him at all times, even for the trials. She said she hadn't been able to relate to this until her fiancé broke their engagement. She tested this verse, thanking the Lord even when she felt as if she were bleeding inside. She burst into a smile and said, "You know, it worked! At first, I didn't *feel* thankful, but after I genuinely thanked God for that situation, He actually *did* make me feel thankful. Now I can take a day at a time, and just thank Him that He is going to work things out."

God's Word gives us many examples of people who thanked God in spite of their deep trouble. Jonah thanked God when he was in the great fish's stomach (Jonah 2:9). Paul and Silas praised God in prison (Acts 16:25). It is easy to praise the Lord when things are going well. But when we praise Him in difficult times, it is then that we are able to manifest Christlikeness. Others cannot understand our attitude, and may, in fact, hunger for what we have.

## KEY 4: A servant attitude develops a humble spirit (Matt. 20:26-28)

One Christmas Eve we were invited to stay overnight with a professor from our college days. He had been the college president and was later president of the National Association of Evangelicals. Before we retired for the night, he and his wife turned back the woolen covers for us. When it occurred to them that I am allergic to wool, he proceeded to take off the covers and remake the bed. I protested, but he would not hear of it. Here was a former college president, a great man, making our bed!

I'll never forget that lesson. He had always manifested a gentle spirit as long as we had known him. We had never seen him display a pushy or a "me first" attitude. This, then, was one of his keys to a Christlike life. His servant attitude revealed his greatness.

Our city inspector is another classic example of the servanthood attitude. In the process of remodeling our home, a workman accidentally hit the gas line. Since no one could identify the source of the leak, a gas company representative came out in a matter of minutes and turned off the entire unit. City inspector Dick Neederhouser arrived a few moments later. Having once worked for the gas company, he tried to tell Stan about how a plumber could repipe our entire gas line over the top of the house. I could see Stan wilt, for neither of us had the slightest idea of what he was talking about. It was suppertime, getting dark, and we had not anticipated such an emergency. As Mr. Neederhouser drove away, we tried to determine what to do. It was two days before payday and we had no money to eat out, no hot water, and no heat (it was the first cold snap of the year). As our conversation progressed, we began to feel more and more dejected. The phone rang. It was Mr. Neederhouser, asking if he could come and fix the pipe so we could have heat and hot water that night! He "just happened" to have at home the exact size of pipe and other materials needed to correct our problem. Within 10 minutes, he was back at our house. After his own long day, he knelt in the dark cold (all we could provide was a flashlight!), cutting away on our pipe with a hacksaw. He then repaired the pipe, turned on our gas unit, and lit the pilots in the house. Who were we, we wondered, out of all the La Mirada residents, that he, the top man as far as the building code was concerned, should fix the gas leak on his own time! We learned that he was a Christian who would not accept any pay for his kindness. We also learned to love his gentle, quiet way. What a beautiful picture of servanthood! It reminded me of Jesus washing the disciples' feet.

I want this servant spirit to permeate my life, going with me everywhere. Being on the faculty of a Bible college does not give me the privilege of breaking into the cafeteria line when students have been waiting for 15 or 20 minutes. In the library or offices, I can take my turn right along with the students and do not need to feel that I should be given special treatment. If I do feel this way, then I have lost that special peace that comes with having Christ's presence with me at all times.

You must discover for yourself how the key of a servant attitude needs to be used in your own life. Perhaps you have a hard time keeping a quiet, humble spirit when you're waiting in traffic, restaurant lines, or the doctor's office.

## KEY 5: Not drawing attention to personal ministry develops self-acceptance (Matt. 6:1; Gal. 6:3-4)

As I hear some "testimonies," I sometimes get the feeling I am listening to the prayers and praise of a Pharisee rather than of a publican. We cannot be judgmental or legalistic about this, but the joy of a ministry can be robbed if there is any hint of "my doing it" rather than the Lord's doing it. Sometimes the results of a seminar or ministry can be kept between the Lord and you because the secret is so precious.

Another way of drawing attention to ourselves and to our ministry is by trying to copy another's life-style or characteristics. God made us as individuals, however, and He wants us to imitate Him, not others. More than once I've heard people comment, "Oh, if only I could be like him," or, "I wish I could have the qualities she has." The African violets in my kitchen don't sigh and say, "Oh, I wish I were like the carnations in the backyard!" Each has its own distinct beauties.

You *can* have the qualities of Christ, but not by coveting or acting like someone else. By spending time alone with the Lord, by learning the lessons He wants to teach *you,* He can give you the Christlike qualities you desire. He will give them to you in His own way, and even make you more beautiful than the person you wish to emulate.

## KEY 6: Letting God fight your battles develops a calm and gentle spirit (2 Chron. 20:17; Ex. 14:14; Ps. 46:10a)

When I was a Bible college student, the great teacher A. W. Tozer was once the guest chapel speaker. His entire talk was about "not being defensive." Though it was an excellent message and much needed in my life, I had not yet arrived at the point in my life's pilgrimage where I could make it work. I blew it every single time. It was not until more than 10 years later that I finally gave up and let the Lord fight my battles. I had to go through many hard lessons and painful experiences before I realized that it doesn't do any good to run around defending yourself.

At last I decided to make a covenant with the Lord. I would let Him do the defending for me. At that time, I was studying what James had to say on the tongue, and nearly every verse seemed to be a sermon just for me. So at midnight one night, I wrote out a covenant in my Bible, with the Lord as my witness, to help me overcome my weakness. I claimed 2 Chronicles 20:17 and Psalm 46:10a as my verses, and with fear and trembling asked God to help me.

The temptation to come to my own defense has never left me—I immediately want to set the whole world straight when an injustice is done (my husband says the Lord will probably make me a traffic cop in the Millennium!) But each time such an experience comes along, I am a little stronger. Why? Because the Lord quickly brings to mind my covenant with Him. As I breathe a prayer for help and quote one of the verses, He gives me the strength to stand silent and let Him fight. When I give my battles to Him, He works in completing the victory. Sometimes He may wait to defend, but He will nevertheless be there. What a thrill to see Him deal with wrongdoing when I don't have to say a word! Letting the Lord fight for me has been a great reward.

It hurts to be put down, to be criticized for something you didn't do (especially when it looked as if you did!). But when you have a clear conscience, it will do you good to remember how God lifted those who have been put down—Joseph, David, and Moses to name a few. When I get discouraged, I like to read about how God used these men in spite of their unjust treatment. This helps me keep my covenant and remember that God is bigger than the situation itself, no matter how absurd it seems.

As I sat at the garden tomb in Jerusalem a few years ago and heard the Rev. Mr. Vander Hoeven, a Jerusalem pastor, speak on John 12:20-43, I was again reminded of Jesus' words, "I must fall and die like a kernel of wheat that falls into the furrows of the earth. Unless I die I will be alone—a single seed. But My death will produce many new wheat kernels—a plentiful harvest of new lives. If you love your life down here—you will lose it. If you despise your life down here—you will exchange it for eternal glory" (vv. 24-25, paraphrased).

I thought then that if I was to be a mirror for the Lord, if I want to bear fruit for other people, I must be willing to fall into the ground and die. For me, this meant being willing to be put down, not to defend myself. My first reaction is to retaliate when an injustice is done, but the fruit of the Spirit and Christ's gentleness surely cannot be manifested in my life when I react in this way. When I think of friends of mine who *do* reflect a calm and gentle spirit, I remember how they respond to criticism. They simply let the Lord take care of it for them.

## Keeping the Keys

Perhaps you are saying, "I will never make it! How can I ever develop such keys as these?" Remember that we will never be perfect. There are many times when I fall short of my keys and have to talk to the Lord about it. The following verse expresses how I felt on a day when I "blew it."

• • •

### I Blew It, Lord

I blew it, Lord, fell flat on my face!
This morning, You revealed
    what's inside me . . .
Utterly wretched—yet,
    You've already taken this sin!
Lift me from these doubts and fears,
How I long to be like You.

My heart reflection is not beautiful.
It's ugly, mean, and hurting.
It wants to strike out.
It stings to look at it—can this be me?
Help me to look at You instead!
Help me to reflect You!

Today I shamefully pick myself up . . .
   painfully,
   sorrowfully . . .
acknowledge a lesson learned.
Hold my hand in Yours, Lord,
   help me go forward,
   and little by little
grow more like You.

• • •

As you develop these keys, remember that they are to be used to keep open the way to becoming more like Jesus Christ, not as gauges with which to judge others. The message of a tract may help you keep your perspectives.

The Lord will let others be honored, and put forward, and keep you hid away in obscurity, because He wants to produce some choice fragrant fruit for His coming glory, which can only be produced in the shade.

He will let others be great, but keep you small. He will let others do a work for Him, and get the credit for it but He will make you work and toil on without knowing how much you are doing; and then to make your work still more precious, He will let others get the credit for the work which you have done, and this will make your reward . . . greater when Jesus comes.

The Holy Spirit will put a strict watch over you, with a jealous love, and will rebuke you for little words and feelings, or for wasting your time, which other Christians never seem distressed over. So make up your mind that God is an infinite Sovereign, and has a right to do as He pleases with

His own. He will not explain to you a thousand things which may puzzle your reason in His dealings with you. He will take you at your word; and if you absolutely sell yourself to be His love slave, He will wrap you in a jealous love, and let other people say and do many things that you cannot do or say.

Settle it forever, then, that you are to deal directly with the Holy Spirit, and that He is to have the privilege of tying your tongue, or chaining your hand, or closing your eyes, in ways that He does not deal with others. Now, when you are so possessed with the living God that you are, in your secret heart, pleased and delighted over this peculiar, personal, private, jealous guardianship and management of the Holy Spirit over your life, you will have found the vestibule of heaven (G. D. Watson, *Living Words,* Good News Publishers, Westchester, Ill.).

"What things were gain to me, those I count loss for Christ" (Phil. 3:7).

• • •

## The Challenge

Here is another one, Lord,
Another rotten situation
which seems totally impossible!

Here it is—
Another chance to become more like You.
Shall I reject it?
and become bitter,
resentful,
less and less like You?
my peace gone?
my joy dissolved into nothingness?
and take the risk of losing Your presence!

Never! A thousand times no!
I cannot give up the glory of Your presence!

But then . . . am I willing to accept this attack . . . head-on?
   all defenses down?
   no holding back?
With all the ammunition of Scripture
And my Lord before me,
   How can I go wrong?

Thank You, Lord for reminding me
   that the conquering is not in the worrying,
     the defending,
     the chattering to others
       of my dismay . . .

   But in the waiting,
     the listening,
     the stillness.
I accept this challenge then . . .
*Full speed ahead, Lord* . . .
*You* will fight my battle while I stand here quiet!
   and because of this trysting place with You,
     because of Your protective balm,
     because of Your words stored away
       in my memory bank,
I will come forth more beautiful than before . . .
Because I will have been made more like *You.*

•  •  •

## Exercise

1. The most difficult problem in my life right now is: _____

_____

_____

2. A verse I can memorize to help me accept this challenge is:

(print it in "picture form")

```



```

3. In conquering this challenge, God will make
    me more like Him by helping me to be

   _____

   _____

4. Memorize the verse.
5. Pray and ask God to:
    a) help you praise Him, even in this situation
    b) give you His view of the situation
    c) guide you to act accordingly.

# Our Application from Listening

## 5

You may already be familiar with your masks—that outward part of yourself you reveal to others. But how well do you know your deep-down attitudes? When God takes your attitudes that are ugly, selfish, and conceited, and transforms them into beautiful, unselfish, servanthood attitudes, you learn that He can use you to enrich the lives of others.

### Your Home

Home is where you usually sleep, eat, bathe, change clothes, and keep your belongings. How can you share it? Through a neighborhood Bible study? Good News Clubs? Crafts 'n Coffee Time? Overnight lodging for a lonely person or a missionary on furlough? Whether you are single or married, your apartment or home can be a radiant testimony for Him.

For nearly 20 years my husband and I lived in parsonages and rented apartments. The first five and a half years at Biola College we lived in a small mobile home. After being in students' lovely apartments we were too embarrassed and crowded to invite them to our home. You can imagine our feelings of sheer joy when we bought our first home, located just a few blocks from the college. We wanted our home to be available to the students—that was to be its primary purpose. But what could we do with all the wall space? After our pastor dedicated our house to the Lord, the decoration of it seemed to be no problem. It was as if God planted ideas in our heads that were different from anything we had ever seen.

One wall is now graced by a large hanging made of drapery material, with an overlay of Pellon on which is printed Psalm 101:2, 6: "I will try to walk a blameless path, but how I need Your help, especially in my own home, where I long to act as I should . . . I will make the godly of the land my heroes and invite them into my home" (LB). On another wall hangs a memorial, a picture taken on our rescue ship out of Egypt. Under the picture are the words, "Acts 7:34a. October 20, 1973. Lest we forget."

These materials have been tools for witness and edification. Long ago, God commanded Joshua to collect 12 stones from the middle of the Jordan River and place them at Gilgal. This was to remind following generations how God had helped the Israelites cross the Jordan on dry land.

Today your apartment or home can have some kind of memorial of what the Lord did on a special day in your life. When children grow up in the home, it is a living testimony to them that God is very much alive and active in that atmosphere.

An apartment we visited recently was charmingly decorated with the occupants' craft of macrame. Creative hangings and several memory boxes filled with items of special occasions added to the testimony of the Lord's goodness. You do not have to be an expert interior decorator to have Bible verses in one form or another throughout your house or apartment. I printed "Wives, fit in with your husband's plans" (1 Peter 3:1a, LB) on a 4" x 6" card and stuck it on the mirror of our dresser. Since it is the first thing I see when I get up in the morning, it helps me with my priorities each day.

Each home or dwelling place needs an affirmation shelf or "warm fuzzie" bulletin board, where birthday cards or thank-you notes can be placed to remind us of someone's love. Many of our cards are so special that we cannot throw them out, so we staple them into a notebook where they can be pondered over on "down" days. They also make wonderful prayer reminders of our loved ones who mean so much.

Every home also needs an area of complete refreshment—where clutter does not exist. Even in a small apartment, a special area can be reserved for this, maybe a reading corner with a stereo and plants—a place where you can relax without having to feel it has to be cleaned up every time you come in the door.

Our living room is the special place in our home, because my husband's favorite reading chair is there. He likes to lean back and throw off his shoes when he comes home from a hard day. I make sure clutter doesn't lie in his line of vision so that he can feel refreshed. Sometimes just a half hour of relaxation in this atmosphere gives him the break he needs before diving into another pile of papers to grade.

How about the yard? Our yard is very small, yet when we moved to this location, we decided to plant flowers of our wedding colors. People look at us in disbelief and sometimes tease, but we don't mind. The flowers are a continual reminder of our love for each other and of our wedding day. In our backyard are trees and plants of the Bible—my husband's idea. We enjoy sharing the flowers and plants in our yard because they belong to the Lord and we want to use them for Him, not just for our enjoyment.

## Your Income

One thing you *don't* need is to have someone tell you how to spend your money. So the only suggestion I have is to listen to the Lord and let *Him* tell you how it should be used—but be sure to *listen!* Sometimes He will change your opinions about your money so you can discover the joy of using part of your income as an investment you never thought of before.

My husband and I believe that we invest in our college students' lives when we take them out for meals or have them in our home. This dips into our budget, of course, but the rewards make it worth the added cost. There is something about sharing a meal that allows the individual to open up, whereas a formal setting might be threatening. When others share prayer requests over meals and when they share in our ministry by praying for us, a discipling bond develops that helps build the relationship Jesus intended for us to have when He said, "For whoever does the will of God, he is My brother and sister and mother" (Mark 3:35).

## Your Car

How can you use your car for the Lord? Afraid it will get muddy and dirty from little children's feet if you load up for Sunday School? How about some outings or times of refreshment with a group with whom you are working? One student husband we know used his car to help another student move— this is true caring for members of the body.

When we bought a van we not only planned to use it for inexpensive once-a-month camping trips, but we wanted to use it for a ministry. We applied for and received an individualized license plate reading "2 READY". Our spare tire is attached to the back, so on the wheel cover we sprayed the reference "1 Cor. 12:20-27," with the words "TO CARE" beneath it. The whole idea, then, was to show how members of the body of Christ can be ready to care for each other. Should the tire cover ever be removed, the plate would still refer to the Lord's coming. Inside the van, we keep a "guest book" which gives the dates and mileage of trips taken with our spiritual children. With our guest book is a photo album which is continually being enlarged by pictures of these spiritual children. This is also a prayer reminder book for us on our vacations and small trips—our spiritual children, namely Biola students, need our prayer support in their ministries.

The license-tire combination has brought many responses, mostly curious, from other motorists. It has also been the source of many questions and opportunities for witness. While waiting for a red light one day, I saw one lady (her husband was driving) pick up her Bible, turn to the passage, follow the verse passage with her fingers, then look back at our car. Many have given positive 'One Way' signs and we know they understand. It is a testimony to others and a continual reminder to us that as members of Christ's body, we are ever caring for one another in some way. This has been a ministry and we wouldn't change it in any way because God has given it to us.

These are a few of the ways in which we've been able to use our vehicle for the Lord. Your situation and opportunities are different from ours, of course. You will be amazed at how He can use your possessions as well as yourself when you accompany your ministry with the servant, rather than the "me-first," attitude.

## Your Abilities

A special friend of ours has an amazing ability to affirm others. She said the Lord gave her this idea while listening to Him. She purchased a small notebook and began writing notes to her college roommate in it. On the first page she entered this note:

> Marci,
>
> After thanking the Lord for you one day, I came upon an interesting thought: 'If you care about that girl so much, why don't you write her?' But you know, I write a note here and a note there, and wonder if you really do know how often my thoughts go to you.
>
> So, I decided to start a "Notes to My Friend, Marci" book. Each day (maybe more often!) I'll add to it, and sometime, anytime—when you feel high, low, or otherwise, just open it up and read it. It will be on my desk—just grab it.
>
> I hope, in this little way, Marci, to let you know how much I love and appreciate you and want to meet your needs.
>
> Love in Christ,
> Bets
> Romans 12:10

In response, her roommate bought a little yellow spiral-bound notebook and her first note answered,

Bets—

You're so special to me! God has blessed me more than I could ever imagine by giving you to me for a friend, helper, "sister," and roomie. What a privilege it is to know and share the same God, too!! Isn't He *super*?!!

This will be your little book of lovenotes to read from me—anytime you want to (if you can find it in my desk clutter!).

I love you so much and just want you to know it!

You're in my thoughts
and prayers (more than you
can imagine!).

Love in great *big* volumes,
Marci

P.S. I chose a yellow notebook because you've been such a bright happy spot in my life! And I'm using green ink because this little book will be sharing with you the small, maybe insignificant (sometimes) ways we will be growing together.

Back and forth these notes fly, each in their own respective notebooks on their own side of the room. These roommates not only communicate better on paper now, but also in one-to-one conversation, all because one of them took the initiative and time to do what she felt the Lord was telling her to do. She listened.

A mother used this "note method" to reach a rebellious daughter. She left little love notes on the girl's pillow after she had left for school. The mother thought the notes were probably being thrown away. But months later, when the daughter finally started to communicate again, she told her mother how much those notes had meant to her. In fact, when the daughter left home for college, she took all those notes with her. They were too precious to throw away.

You have probably become aware of the fact that in your

quiet times you will be making some new discoveries. Your quiet time with the Lord will begin to affect every area of your life, and inevitably cause you to reach out to others, maybe even change your life-style. In some way, the Lord will be able to use you as a channel for blessing others, whether it be through your talents, your vocation, or your possessions. Are you willing to be vulnerable enough to risk sharing your life so that others can grow? Christ was.

## Exercise

1. Ask the Lord to reveal to you what unique qualities or possessions of yours He would like to use. Then *listen*. (You may have to listen for a few days.)

2. List any qualities or possessions you feel you would be willing to share in an obedient life-style. Then next to each item, write one way which you feel the Lord might be telling you how to use it for Him. Be specific.

1.

2.

3.

4.

5.

6.

7.

8.

9.

10.

# Training for More Sensitive Listening

## 6

Alone in an empty parking lot, I felt a sick feeling in the bottom of my stomach as one of our van's tires defiantly hissed out its last bit of air. The van slumped on the tire rim and my spirit slumped with it. "Lord," I thought, "what lesson do You want me to learn through this?"

I walked to the nearby gas station. At this early hour of the morning, the attendants were not too busy and the manager said he would come and help. He changed the tire, but not before he had noticed our license plate which reads, "2 READY."

"You weren't quite ready for this, were you?" he said, laughing.

"No," I responded, "but the license plate doesn't refer to flat tires. It's talking about the Lord's coming."

He nodded and smiled, and in that short exchange I felt that it was an opportunity to witness that might never have come without a flat tire. Sure, the flat tire could have upset my entire day. Sure, it scared me. Changing a tire on a regular car is enough to terrify any woman alone, but on our Chevy 20 van—a *truck?* Later that day, we had to buy a new tire, but through it all, I tried to keep a sensitive ear to the Lord, asking

Him to tell me what He wanted me to learn through this lesson.

The next morning during my quiet time, I wrote down five things for which I could thank the Lord concerning the flat tire. (1) It happened in a parking lot and not on the freeway while I was driving. (2) A service station was next door and the manager put a spare on for me. I might have had to walk for blocks. (3) He charged me only $4.00. He could have charged me $14.00. (4) He noticed our "2 READY" license plate so that there was an opportunity for witness. (5) The Lord helped me not to get upset, but to take it in stride.

Number 5 was a major lesson, because one of my biggest problems is that I'm a great "prayer closet promiser." I promise the Lord that I will do certain things, but when situations occur to prove those promises, I find it hard to keep them. One of the things I have had to ask the Lord to do is to make me strong in crisis situations. This lesson was just a beginning of what was to follow, but the Lord helped me to meet the challenges head-on.

The lesson of the flat tire was one of many I've learned in God's schools. His schools for you may be of a different kind. You may now be in one of His schools of faith, suffering, endurance, or of uncertainty. It may be a refresher course in one of His schools, a reminder from the Master Teacher that there are still more lessons to be learned before you complete the course. As I look back over the three schools I have attended recently—the School of Grief, the School of Endurance, and the School of Dependence—I am amazed and excited at the extensive learning activity with the Lord that has taken place.

## The School of Grief

Many of my letters to the Lord during the late months of 1976 discuss death or grief. In late September and early November, two of our friends went to be with the Lord. Then in December, a near relative unexpectedly entered His presence. During this time, I was fully aware that my closest Biola friend of 10 years, Inez Gooden, was to answer God's summons at any time. Through our friendship I was to realize an anticipation for heaven that I had never experienced before.

Inez' quick laugh and gentle spirit had endeared her to me and we became fast friends. We were on the same wavelength and had many things in common. We felt refreshed from just being with each other. During my seminary days, we spent choice moments at the library desk where she had been such a servant to so many. With our husbands we had visited Catalina Island. We had assisted in robing the faculty for commencement each year. When the news came that she had cancer and was not expected to live longer than a few months, I was at first frightened, not knowing what to say.

We fully expected Inez to be the fourth of our loved ones to die in a matter of months. Then the Lord unexpectedly took another loved one home which was to further deepen our sensitivity to those in grief.

We had enjoyed celebrating Christmas day with Frank and Laura-Eloise Ray, our "spiritual parents." After a few weeks of intense testing, it was discovered that Frank had cancer of the pancreas and might live as long as three months. Eleven days later he was gone. He had been one of my husband's closest friends and advisors. We had known him for almost 19 years; Stan had baptized him in our church in Hawaii. It was unbelievable that this had happened, especially as we waited for Inez to hear her summons from the Lord.

During these days we seemed to approach the gates of heaven in our quiet times with the Lord. Tears flowed uncontrollably at the most unexpected times and I could sense in Stan a rising anger that was not to be so easily released. Because of this, I read Joyce Landorf's *Mourning Song* (Revell, 1974) and came to a new understanding of the phases of the acceptance of death. But I was haunted by the thought that each loved one taken seemed to be closer to us than the last one. This caused me to ask the Lord, "Are You preparing me for the death of Stan, or are You preparing Stan for my homegoing?" I began to feel as though I was being morbid and preoccupied with my own death.

About this time God arranged to bring Joyce Landorf and me together for a short, meaningful encounter. I thanked her for her honesty in her book, *Mourning Song,* and her first reaction was, "And whom have you lost?" Briefly I related that Stan was to preach the memorial service for Frank, his spiritual father, in just three days and that he was hurting deeply inside. We talked for a few more minutes, then separated.

I wanted to ask her a dozen more questions but it was not the time or place, so a few days later I wrote Joyce a letter. I expressed my feelings of hypocrisy as I was teaching the "Roles of Women" class on the outside, trying to act as though all was well, and on the inside feeling all torn up. I was interested in finding out how her husband, Dick, had reacted to the death of their son David, and wanted to know how I could help Stan with his hurt. I was surprised to find in the mail a few days later a letter from Joyce with encouragement and insights. She had written,

Your husband's behavior is terribly, terribly normal but I can understand how it frightens you. Stan's anger, which is beginning to bubble and may surface, is no problem to the Lord. The Lord gave us the emotion of anger and it will not shock the Lord.

If I were his wife, I would simply be praying that God will bring him to a point of verbalizing the anger in some manner. If he chooses to verbalize his anger on you, you might end up a punching bag, but remember as it is happening that it desperately needs to be cleared out of his system or it will turn into bitterness and that is an infection that rarely is healed. . . .

The world says that we must return to normal as quickly as possible after the death of a loved one, but we who experience this kind of loss know that many times nothing can ever be "normal" again. You have to build a new normal, a new way of living and turn your full attention to yourself and to those who live around you. God never wastes experiences, so I am sure He intends to use all of this in your lives.

Just about the time of Frank's tests, Inez's husband, Gerry, told me that Inez was planning her own memorial service and wanted me to be the organist. I protested, for I hadn't played the organ for five years. But Gerry assured me that all would go well, and because of Inez' expressed wish and my love for her, I consented. For two months death glared up at me from the organ keys as I practiced the songs Inez wanted to be played in remembrance of her. When the sudden news of Frank's homegoing came, I stopped practicing. I was pre-occupied with death. Yet during this time, my quiet times with the Lord were a way of release and healing.

• • •

## The School of Grieving

You took him suddenly, Lord,
    and we stood in breathless wonder
    at the speed of his homegoing.
He is the fourth in a series
    of about one each month
    to keep an appointment with You,
    and there is yet another
    who awaits her summons.

Lord, I am bogged down
    from the ache of losing them.
They are with You,
    and for that I am grateful.
But we still miss them,
Their places are empty here.

I had no idea
    that grief is so searing;
    it dulls my senses,
    numbs my rejoicing spirit,
    brings forth unexpected torrents of tears
    from a bottomless well.

Lord, what lesson have I not yet learned
    that You should allow grief upon grief,
    when the last wound has not yet healed?
Whatever You want to teach me,
    please teach me quickly,
    for I am weary, worn, tired of death.
I long to graduate from this course in mourning
    so I can be joyously fruitful again.

Lord, You have said
    "Weeping endures for a night,
    but joy comes in the morning" (Ps. 30:5).
End my night, Lord,
    for I feel like such a hypocrite,
    smiling on the outside,
    pretending all is right with the world,
    when inside I'm torn apart,
    trying to mend my broken spirit.

I trust in You for whatever lessons
    You have yet to teach me.
I am a willing and eager student,
    who is sometimes slow;
    so please be gentle with me,
    in this school of grieving.

• • •

On March 1 Inez's husband Gerry called to tell us, "The vigil is over."

Inez's memorial service was the most unusual I have ever attended. Dr. George Simms spoke on "The Legacy of a Quiet Spirit." I was so moved by his message that when the service was over I wanted to be alone. I walked slowly to the car and sat there for a long time. The next morning in my quiet time, my feelings flowed through my pen:

• • •

Oh, my Lord,
I felt like I was in Your Almighty presence last night
   in Inez Gooden's memorial service.
I wanted to be alone for hours
   just to reflect on the entire service
      and its effect on me.

You confirmed through George Simms
   what You have been teaching me:
The *true* test and strength of Your church on this earth,
   should tests and persecutions come,
   will not be in how important we are
      if we are known,
      if we have degrees,
      how far we have traveled,
   but in a gentle, quiet spirit.
   Our strength will hold in this,
because our spiritual fiber will have been strengthened
   through *listening* to You
      in the development of this trait.

No one ever taught me how to listen to You.
   The church did not teach me.
   Professors never taught me.
   They taught me how to *talk* to You . . .
      but not how to listen.

And what I need to do is to *listen*. . . .
   I make dozens of decisions daily,
      and without the gentle, quiet spirit of listening,
   I stumble from needless errors.

These quiet minutes and hours with You
   are the priceless, rare investments which will pay off
      in the gentle spirit so precious to You.
Oh, God, I love You and ask to be more like You.

• • •

## Compassionate Christ

Lean on Me, child, and cry,
   I know your heart is broken . . .
I called your loved one home today,
   She is with Me.

Look to Me, child, and trust,
   I am acquainted with grief . . .
I welcomed your precious one
   to a home far better than earth.

Hold on to Me, child,
   I see your tear-washed face . . .
I know the searing of your soul,
   and will ease your pain.

Cling to Me, child,
   I know you loved her,
But I loved her more . . .
   and died that she could be here with Me.

Keep your eyes on Me, child,
   I will not abandon you . . .
No words can describe
   the peace I will give you.

Be comforted, My child,
   Your loved one is rejoicing in My presence,
   Her entrance into heaven was accompanied
   with triumphant exultation!
   . . . and because of the beauty of her lifelong legacy,
   I want you to love Me more,
   and to watch for My coming.

For I am coming for you, My child,

and you will be with Me,
and see your loved one again,
where you will know no tears, death, or loneliness.

I love you, dear child
and know your hurt . . .
So lean on Me, and cry.

*—in memory of*
*beloved Inez*
*now with Jesus*
*March 1, 1977*

## The School of Endurance

Whenever I ask to be more like the Lord, He takes me up on it. Before Inez's memorial service, I had asked the Lord, "If it is Your will, please do not entrust me with any more grieving, but lead me in new lessons you want me to learn." So the school of grief was apparently over, at least for now.

The very next day, in the doctor's office, my entrance into the School of Edurance began. For several months there had been a slight bulge in my side, and after an examination, the doctor hospitalized me for tests. These tests were not only a true proof of endurance, but they were also a lesson to show me that like tumors, sin must be removed, and hurt always accompanies that.

After a week of testing, our doctor decided to do a laparoscopy, a procedure in which a small instrument is inserted through an incision in the navel to scan the inside of the abdomen. The doctor had warned my husband and me that if tumors were present, he would probably perform a hysterectomy. We both OK'd the operation, but I was not expecting a mass exit of organs.

• • •

### The Patient's Paraclete*
Come sit on my bed, Lord
and be very real.

The hospital staff won't mind
   if You're with me.

Just reassure me, Lord
   and hold me.
The test today
   is one of the worst, they say.

Linger here with me, Lord.
   I need Your presence
in these unfeeling rooms
   of steel and metal.

Touch me with Your peace, Lord,
   and let it flow through my spirit
Out to others, unconsciously,
   so that today it can drown out
      my anxieties.

You know my trembling, Lord,
   how my heart panics,
   and my body quakes,
at the very thought of conscious probing,
   and I feel so terribly alone.

So, Lord, go with me in my wheelchair
   through those halls and down that elevator,
     to that dreaded room of cold aloofness,
   where icy instruments penetrate
     the most delicate of my tissues.

Enable me to gather up the shreds of fear
   and calmly hold them in my heart,
While You hold me in Your hand.

---

*paraclete—called to one's side

• • •

The night before surgery can be one of the loneliest in a person's life. After visiting hours were over at the hospital, the unwelcome visitors, Fear and Dread, came and sat by my side. Then the telephone rang—it was our church elder. This angel of mercy prayed with me over the phone and calmed the fears I had. After we finished talking, I felt I was in God's hands. My body was His and He was to use it as He saw fit.

The next morning my quiet time with the Lord was especially sweet. My regular devotional reading was from Psalm 63, so when I got to these verses, I claimed them as special from the Lord to me.

When I remember Thee on my bed
I meditate on Thee in the night watches.
For Thou hast been my help,
And in the shadow of Thy wings I sing for joy.
My soul clings to Thee;
Thy right hand upholds me (Ps. 68:6-8, NASB).

Then I said to the Lord, "Today is surgery, Lord, and I need You here with me in a very special way. Please hide me under Your wings. I commit my body, soul, and spirit to you for whatever happens. I love You, regardless of the outcome." The tests of the previous week had just been an introduction to the School of Endurance. Surgery and the convalescence which was to follow would provide many new opportunities for lessons and tests never faced before.

• • •

### Exposure
Here in the hospital, Lord,
    there is no rushing,
        no running,
        no hiding
    from obvious difficulties.

In here, wrongs are righted—deliberately.
   Tests are run, skin is cut
      and the offender is taken out.

It hurts, Lord, even before the cutting begins,
   to look the culprit in the face—
   and know it must be eliminated.

It's like sin, isn't it, Lord,
   that has crept in unknowingly,
   and suddenly it's there, growing,
          crippling my ministry.

Then, in taking it out,
   You scan my innermost motives
   and use instruments (Your Word and people)
     to test and penetrate deeply
     until the imbedded enemy is exposed,
              severed,
         and destroyed forever.

Thank You for teaching me, Lord,
   that in Your hospital of life,
     *endurance* in testing is necessary
     in order to make me *aware* of foreign material.
There must be probing, hurting, and dislodgement
     of the cause of weakness
     so I can be cleansed again to be used of You.

●   ●   ●

Sometimes in the midst of learning a lesson, we don't even understand ourselves. We feel like we're groping in the dark.

The doctors found a number of tumors and performed the promised surgery. It had not occurred to me that a major operation causes tremendous shock not only to the body, but to the emotions as well. And I was getting my emotional trauma confused with my spiritual condition.

For a week after surgery, I wrote nothing in my quiet time notebook. This void was perhaps caused by a terrible nightmare which the anesthesia may have induced. I thought it was so evil that I wondered if the Lord had allowed it to test or discipline me. Most of my conscious moments between visitors and pain shots were spent trying to analyze what was going on between the Lord and me, and just listening to Him. I tried to talk to Him, but felt so much in the fog from being drugged that I could not consistently be in a communicative state. Both my body and emotions felt numb. At times I felt like a whimpering child just after a paddling session. Yet, I knew my heavenly Father loved me and even snuggled me to Himself in the moments of deepest hurting.

Because of my hospital experience I understand tremendously important lessons. When people are in a hospital bed of pain, we are not to expect them to make leaps of spiritual growth. I also learned that misuse of Scripture can hurt more than physical pain. Sermonizing and Scripture verses come across like a blast of arctic air to a patient when he needs the warmth of support and encouragement. Scripture reading requested by the patient is one thing, but being commanded to "cheer up" and "be strong" only creates guilt when the patient feels depressed and weak.

After coming home, a full week went by before I looked at the date in my quiet time notebook. I realized I had to come to terms with the Lord and be honest about my feelings. He then began to teach me on that day new lessons in His School of Dependence.

## The School of Dependence

In the hospital, I had had thoughts of, "Lord, You have plopped me into a corner of absolute helplessness. The doctor has said, 'No work, no travel, *no nothing,* for two weeks.' Lord, You know how this cuts off all teaching commitments I have made." I argued with Him, and then had to accept the fact that He was trying to teach me that I had to give my husband back to the Lord, even in team-teaching situations.

I had to give our home back to God, and not be upset about how it looked when we had our classes there. I had to turn our seminars over to Him, especially those in which our original Bible games were involved. Now this was a big lesson for me, because I like to be organized, to the point of being fussy. So I wrote,

Lord, I've been picky, I've been proud . . .

—too picky to let others handle my homemade games, afraid they might mess them up,

—too proud that they wouldn't be taught in the right way . . .

—afraid that pressure on Stan would hurt his teaching so much he would lose rapport.

Thank you, Lord, for teaching me that I must trust You for these things, that I am helpless, and that in my weakness, You can be glorified. Thank you for teaching me that when I'm helpless, You make the decisions.

Lord, about this void of the past week. Why the awful nightmare in the hospital? Why did I feel that You were punishing me? Why did You seem so far away, even when I tried to communicate with You? Was it because I felt hurt that You had allowed this to happen to me? Yet, I felt You had protected and loved me through it all. Forgive me, Lord, forgive my hurt. I guess that during the dark week after surgery, I just kind of closed You out. I hurt emotionally because You allowed it all to happen so suddenly, and I hurt spiritually because of the evil nightmare which made me feel You had left me."

That week, to me, was one of intense listening to the Lord. I have been deeply impressed with what Oswald Chambers says about the "Discipline of Heeding":

Watch where God puts you into darkness, and when you are there keep your mouth shut. Are you in the dark just now in your circumstances, or in your life with God? Then remain quiet. If you open your mouth in the dark, you will talk in the wrong mood: darkness is the time to listen. Don't talk to other people about it; don't read books to find out the reason for the darkness, but listen and heed. If you talk to other people, you cannot hear what God is saying. When you are in the dark, listen, and God will give you a very precious message for someone else when you get into the light.[1]

Often in the School of Dependence God wants to teach us to receive graciously. This was another lesson which was to be learned before I got well. Stan's students came to the house to help in unexpected ways. They prepared meals, washed dishes, scrubbed the floor, cleaned the refrigerator, vacuumed the carpet, did the laundry, ironed, washed the car, trimmed the hedge, weeded, mowed the lawn, ran errands, did shopping, typed, etc.

God taught me to accept these expressions of love and spiritual gifts and revealed to me that a "servant-spirit" attitude was more important than being well known. This is what we had been trying to teach the students and now it was coming home. With a choked-up throat, I told the Lord, "You have helped us see that Your principles we have been trying to teach have finally been learned." But it was also my responsibility to accept these gifts lovingly, and not to reject them. Acceptance can be difficult, especially when we are taught all our lives not to accept "charity." But God teaches us to be gentle and quiet in receiving the gifts of others, and to give a genuine "thank-you" in return.

## Insure Maximum Benefit from God's Lessons

How can we benefit from God's teaching in His classrooms? Many lessons slip by simply because we do not realize that they are lessons God wants us to learn. We sit and sulk, and say, "Why, Lord, have You allowed this to happen to me?" thereby rejecting the lesson and the joy of graduation from the course. If we sincerely say, "OK, Lord, what is it You want me to learn?" we can gain insights from the Lord, because all the while He is there.

How can you solidify lessons and follow them up?

*Write down the situation that God allowed.* For example, the last few situations God allowed me to be in were: the deaths of five close friends and a hospitalization, all within six months. You might be in a situation of waiting, of stepping out in faith, or of suffering. You might be experiencing some deep hurt of rejection. Write down your actual situation. Then follow through on the remainder of these steps. They will help you become aware of how you are growing.

*Write down what you learned from that situation.* What has helped me the most in learning the lessons God wants to teach me is to write down the things I feel He has impressed on me. Knowing what these things are comes through listening. In the quiet moments, after I have read the Scripture, finished praying, and written my letter to Him, I will close my Bible, close my eyes, and concentrate on the Lord. I say something like, "Lord, what is it You want for me today? I'm listening to You right now. In this situation that You have allowed me to be in, what lessons do You want me to learn?" Or, "What have You taught me through this lesson? Help me to be able to crystallize this right now."

As I sit and think on Him, He impresses on my mind His thoughts. On previous days I may have had fleeting insights which soon were gone because I was so busy doing something else. It may have occurred to me that the Lord was trying to teach me something, but I never wrote it down. The quiet time is the time to listen and to write. The joy of it is in relaxing and *not hurrying.* Don't rush the Lord. He will impress thoughts on your mind if you give Him time.

One week after my hospitalization, I wrote at the top of a page, *Lessons I Learned from this Hospitalization.* There were eight.

1. Sharpened listening to the Lord. This was my time to be quiet and allow my Master Teacher to impress on my mind what He wanted me to learn. It was not a time to talk or to search for a reason *why* He was teaching me. It was a time to

simply accept the impressions He was engraving on my heart and life, so that when full health returned, I could better minister to others.

2. Complete dependence on Him. As a result, to commit my pickiness to the Lord concerning our seminars, our team-teaching classes, and especially my clean house.

Even before the semester began, Stan and I had planned the Tuesday night of my hospital stay. We had arranged to have our Roles of Women/Roles of Men classes to be held in our home on that date. We felt that the Lord had planted this idea in our minds, and He knew ahead of time that we would *really* need the guest speakers, one of whom was president of Biola, right at this time!

It is only normal for a faculty wife to feel somewhat threatened when the president of the college is to visit. But to be helpless, in the hospital, unable to clean the house as I would have liked, and unable to welcome our guests, was devastating! I had to commit this to the Lord and ask Him to take care of the entire situation. As it turned out, the students cleaned the house and were on hand, along with Stan, to welcome our guests, and they got along just fine without me!

3. Give Stan back to God in our team-teaching ministry. God could use him without me. He really *is God's!*

• • •

## Dependence

You've put me here—in this corner,
    utterly helpless, dependent on You.

Unexpected surgery,
    a doctor's orders of absolute quiet,
    and I am a victim of uselessness, it seems.

But You have allowed this
    and I feel ambivalence—
    a special joy in being cuddled to Your side for this time,
    and a hurt for having to learn some new lessons right now.
        Why is it that lessons come so hard?

Why can't I accept your discipline graciously,
　　without tears?

For 23 years we have worked as a team, my husband and I.
　　Now, for weeks, he must work through details without me,
　　　　And it stings to see him bear the brunt of it.
　　　　　　I must be willing to give up my share of the work.
To be patient . . . to be quiet . . .
　　Lord, I'm learning all of this,
　　but there is more You want of me this time,
and as I linger daily in this special private arena of
　　Your Presence,
　　help me to learn Your lessons willingly and joyfully,
　　　　For I belong to You,
　　　　　　and everything I have is Yours.

· · ·

4. To see the blossoming of the "servant-spirit" of many of
the students. This was a real joy.

· · ·

### Blooming of Servanthood

Because of my helplessness,
　　they came, Lord,
　　　　to share in my husband's ministry—
　　and their response
　　　　overwhelmed me,
　　　　humbled me,
　　　　submerged me in wonder.
Your servant-spirit was reflected, Lord,
　　in their 20th-century menial tasks of
　　　　cooking, washing dishes,
　　　　laundry, ironing,
　　　　cleaning, dusting,
　　　　mowing the lawn,
　　　　washing the car,
　　　　running errands . . .

whatever they could
   to make the load lighter
   for my teacher-husband.

I was moved, Lord, by their constant prayers and notes,
   repeated hospital visits—
   and some were sentinels through the uncertain hours of
     surgery.
They needed to use these gifts, Lord,
   to reveal Your servant-spirit.
They did what they could
   to say "I love you" in deed.

Lord, how I thank You for this lesson
   of complete dependence—
     because it helped these choice students
      early in their ministries,
      to learn the joy of serving,
      to realize that to become a leader,
        one must first learn to serve.

• • •

5. God was in complete control. When our church elder phoned me the night before surgery, I confessed to him that I really felt I might be next on God's appointment list. I knew I had to also submit this to the Lord to have complete peace about the situation. The Lord's timing in teaching me this lesson was about as subtle as a freight train. He had allowed me to be admitted into the hospital *less than 24 hours after Inez Gooden's memorial service,* and she had been the closest to me of the five friends who had died during the last six months. The doctor's belief that I had tumors which might have to be removed only confirmed the feeling that I was next. God confronted me with my helplessness and forced me to submit to His timing.

6. Those who had gone through the deepest of hurts had ministered to us the most effectively.

Joyce Landorf had ministered to me in real comfort and insight because she had also been through the experience of losing loved ones. It was practical advice, not a sermon to make me feel worse. Her words were a real encouragement as the School of Grief overlapped into the Schools of Endurance and Dependence.

Gerry Gooden, whose wife had died just 15 days before, ministered with a sensitivity born from his own sorrow. There he was, in the midst of his grief-work, sticking close to Stan through the hours of surgery. He had been through dark hospital hours himself, and knew what they were. I will never forget his supportive hug of reassurance as I was carted to the surgery room.

Laura-Eloise Ray, a Christian homemaker who had watched with agony all the tests her husband had had to endure before cancer was discovered, came to our home to minister after I returned from the hospital. She prepared meals, did dishes, and just cheered us on. She was a tremendous testimony of strength in using her grief creatively to support someone else in their need.

These people taught me that only by *going through a situation* such as this will I have the sensitivity to help others. My "ministry" to others will be superficial unless I can truly empathize.

7. Support and counsel from God's people can make the weakest walls of doubt become fortifications of courage. After surgery, I searched in vain for a magazine, a book, a brochure, *anything* that would help me understand what was happening to me physically and emotionally. Nothing seemed to have been written on the subject. After days of bewilderment and fruitless calls to the doctor's office, I finally succumbed to a world of ignorance and pain.

Then, in answer to a silent cry to the Lord, Biola College physician and our dear friend, Dick Nollmeyer, volunteered to come over to the house and answer any questions we had. Even after a busy day, this gentle and godly man patiently drew diagrams and answered questions that had been nagging us for weeks. He assured me that the emotional jolt of such a major surgery was not to send me on guilt trips in my spiritual life, and that right at this time, my own evaluation of myself was not too valid.

The prayer support of people who did not even know me proved powerful too. Cards came from people whom I had never met. My hospital roommate was a Christian. She had been released shortly after I had returned from the recovery room. A few days later, she wrote to tell me that she had called several sources to put my name on a prayer chain, one being a Christian TV program. I was humbled and yet so grateful for this intercession.

8. The Lord was gracious in not allowing me to know ahead of time of the impending surgery and of the tumors that were present. He gave me peace in submitting my body to Him for what He wanted to do.

These then were some of the lessons that made a tremendous impact on my spiritual pilgrimage. They were to make me stronger for future ministry. Much to my surprise, however, one of our former students, now also teaching at Biola, wrote 16 lessons that *she* had learned from my hospitalization experience. A Talbot seminary student, a close friend of ours, also wrote in a beautiful letter to the Lord Jesus what He had taught him through this same experience. Why my experience should have brought lessons to their minds is beyond me, but it showed a sensitivity to the Lord that deeply moved us. If an experience of mine can touch other lives in a way that makes Christ more real to them, then I am grateful.

*Share with someone else the lessons learned.* Sharing is so important in stabilizing the learning situation. It helps you remember more clearly what happened and gives you more strength and encouragement for the next test. It helps you remember that God was there through the entire lesson—He did not step out of the classroom when the hardest tests came. New insights into your own spiritual life can be gained. You will soon discover that as you write down what you have learned from your lesson, and share that with someone else, your spiritual fiber is stronger than before.

*Ask the Lord what He wants you to do.* The Lord showed me that He wanted me to act on some of the lessons I had learned, to strengthen and encourage others. He wanted me to respond to the blossoming servant-spirit of our students, to show gratefulness and appreciation for their expressions of love to us. These students did not *have* to do those menial tasks—it was a sacrifice of time on their part.

One lesson the Lord taught me about listening occurred in the doctor's office a few weeks after my operation. I was in tears after having heard the advice of a dozen people, some saying I was up too soon, others saying I was not up soon enough.

"Listen to *me*," my doctor gently ordered. "I know your insides better than anyone else; I saw them and they were a complete mess. If you do what I say, everything will be all right."

How beautiful the analogy to what the Lord says. He wants us to listen to *Him,* not to the many voices around us. "I know your insides," He says, "and they were a spiritual mess. Listen to *Me,* and I will instruct you."

*Ask the Lord how you can thank Him in the test.* We are not unfeeling. God has given us emotions; He has given us tears. When we hurt, we can lean on Him and cry. But we can also turn around and praise Him that it wasn't a worse situation. I could thank the Lord immediately that the tumors removed from my body were benign, and that I wasn't number six on the death list.

Hurts in the training the Lord gives us make us more sensitive to Him. Learning these lessons—going through these lessons in God's schools—are just ways of getting to know our Master Teacher better. The way we become more like Christ is to accept the learning situation and His lessons with a humble, teachable spirit.

## Exercise 6

1. Describe briefly in writing a situation in which God is allowing you to learn lessons right now.

2. Write down lessons you are learning from this situation. When you have finished with your regular quiet time activities, sit a few moments with your eyes closed and ask the Lord what lesson He wants you to learn from this situation.
3. Share this lesson with one other person—someone who can keep your confidence.
4. Ask the Lord what He wants you to do or how you can act on it. Write this down. Then *do* act on it.
5. Ask the Lord how you can thank Him in this. Write down a "thank-You, Lord" for this situation.

(Keep these pages in a separate place in your quiet time notebook. Perhaps a "Lessons Learned" section would be helpful.)

This is merely a guide to help you get through your courses with the Master Teacher in a more beneficial way. You may add any steps you wish to help you grow.

---

[1] Oswald Chambers, *My Utmost for His Highest.* (New York: Dodd, Mead and Company, 1935), p. 45.

# Our Reflections from Listening

## 7

When Jesus sent out the disciples in groups of two (Mark 6:7), He knew the benefits of having a special companion and of doing things together which help both individuals grow in Christlikeness because they are ministering to each other. While the foregoing chapters of this book have dealt with our individual relationship with God, this chapter consists of exercises whereby we can allow someone else to help us grow. It can be used with your prayer partner, college roommate, or spouse. These exercises, however, are not meant to be a substitute for your personal listening times with God.

These exercises are designed to be used on a daily basis. A new exercise can be used each day of the month and then repeated the next month with different applications, *or* principles which you or your partner have discovered.

The greatest value will be gained only if the persons involved can relate to each other honestly. *Each partner needs to recognize that he must commit himself to the other for mutual spiritual growth because these exercises will demand time, effort, and perseverance.* There must also be a basis of love so that each can challenge, confront, and encourage the other without putting a strain on the relationship. This is definitely *not* for casual acquaintances, new friends, or people who see each other once or twice a week.

The exercises are numbered for each day of the month. A Scripture verse or passage is to be read first for meditation and quiet reflection. The second part is a response which opens the door for in-depth communication and sharing. Occasionally, options will be given for applying or discovering a biblical guideline. As each partner supports the other, the godly quality should become evident in each life.

READ:Colossians 1:9-10         First Day

RESPOND:  To strengthen your relationship, pray for God's will to reach *one* of these goals *this month*.
1. Assign one day this month to be for one partner only; assign one day of the month to be for the other partner only. These days are to be planned for refreshment.
2. Arrange one room or area in your home, apartment, or room as a refuge for solitude, Bible study, or prayer activities.
3. Read one day each week a chapter in a devotional book, or a Christian magazine article for spiritual enrichment.
4. Write your own goal.

REFLECT:  God's will

•  •  •

READ:  Proverbs 16:3         Second Day

RESPOND:  Pray together for today's work and this month's plans. James 2:18. In what way will I demonstrate *my* faith today?
      —studying    —working    —traveling
       —cleaning house    —other

REFLECT:  commitment

• • •

READ: Matthew 5:1-16        Third Day

RESPOND:
1. Thank your partner for one of the characteristics mentioned in this passage which you see in *his/her* life.
2. Choose one of these blessings which you want to see manifested in your life.
3. What is needed to qualify for a blessing?
4. Pray for each other to have an opportunity to express this obedience in your life today.

REFLECT: obedience

• • •

READ: Colossians 3:16-17        Fourth Day

RESPOND:
1. Select a hymn, psalm, or song which will refresh your partner spiritually.
2. Find in the words of the song an expression that will encourage you today.
3. Do one of these three activities:
   a. Sing the song together.
   b. Memorize one verse of the song.
   c. Meditate on the meaning of the words of one verse.

REFLECT: edification in song

• • •

READ: Mark 10:45        Fifth Day

RESPOND:
1. Discuss with your partner how each of you can in a special way serve the other today.
   Examples: washing your partner's car; fixing a favorite dish; doing your partner's chores.

2. Pray for each other to minister in this way.
3. *Do it without expecting anything in return.*

REFLECT: servanthood

• • •

READ: 1 Peter 3:8-9                Sixth Day

RESPOND:
1. Remind your partner when he or she last returned a kind act for an injury.
2. Identify an area where *you* have currently been hurt.
3. How can you give a "blessing" in return for this hurt?
4. Pray for each other for courage to carry out this confirmation of love.
5. Plan for a specific time to fulfill this confirmation.

REFLECT: loving submission

• • •

READ: 2 Peter 1:5-8              Seventh Day

RESPOND: Select one quality in this list and ask your partner to pray that this quality will be evident in your life today.

REFLECT: knowing God better

• • •

READ: Hebrews 13:1-2, 1 Peter 4:9 Eighth Day

RESPOND:
1. Ask yourselves, when was the last time we demonstrated Christian hospitality?
2. Ask God for ways to obey Him in this area.

REFLECT: hospitality

READ: 1 Thessalonians 5:14-17     Ninth Day

RESPOND:
1. Different needs demand different responses. Each partner should name one need in his or her own life.
2. List some ways to meet this need and discuss which
   would be best.
3. Pray for God's help to meet one need in your partner's
   life today.

REFLECT: flexibility in meeting needs

• • •

READ: 1 Timothy 4:7b-8     Tenth Day

RESPOND:
1. Ask your partner in what area you need to develop discipline.
   Examples: —time management
             —eating habits
             —rest/refreshment
2. Decide on steps to improve.
3. Write a reminder on your calendar one week from today
   to evaluate yourself on self-discipline.
4. Request God's help to reflect godliness in self-discipline.

REFLECT: discipline

• • •

READ: 2 Corinthians 12:8-9a     Eleventh Day

RESPOND:
1. Identify one limitation in your own life and share it
   with your partner.
2. Ask God to:
   a. help you to accept this limitation;

b. reveal His power today through this restriction.

REFLECT: acceptance of limitations

• • •

READ: Isaiah 30:15            Twelfth Day

RESPOND:
1. Plan a definite time today for absolute quietness and solitude. Write it down, and share it with your partner.
2. Ask God to help you keep this appointment so that you can be refreshed with renewed confidence.
3. Check up on each other.

REFLECT: quietness

• • •

READ: Ephesians 4:31-32, LB     Thirteenth Day

RESPOND:
1. Ask your partner to identify for you the last time you manifested one of these traits: bad temper, harsh words, dislike of others, quarrelsomeness. Pray, asking God's forgiveness and help to stop responding in that way.
2. Have your partner identify for you the last time you were: kind, tenderhearted, or forgiving. Pray for each other, asking that these characteristics will be evident in your lives today.

REFLECT: forgiveness

• • •

READ: 1 Thessalonians 5:16-18     Fourteenth Day

RESPOND:
1. Thank your partner for one quality you appreciate in his or her life.

2. Pray, thanking God for the blessing your partner is to you in your life.

REFLECT: thanksgiving

• • •

READ: Psalm 1:1-3                    Fifteenth Day

RESPOND:
1. Discuss together any pressures, however subtle they may be, that come from ungodly sources (people, TV, etc.) that might affect our godly walk.
2. Share together one delightful promise or guideline from God's Word that will help you follow the Lord more closely today.
3. In what area of our relationship do we want to claim God's blessing for prosperity? (Isa. 30:15; 2 Chron. 20:15, 17)
   Examples: ministry at church, testimony to unsaved, family relationships.

REFLECT: prosperity

• • •

READ: Isaiah 40:29-31                Sixteenth Day

RESPOND:
1. When was the last time you were tired and exhausted? Pray for God's strength and endurance for what you face today.
2. Suggest to your partner specific ways each can trust God for refreshment and endurance.
   Examples:
   a. Find God's refreshment in
        quietness      reading      singing.
   b. Discipline yourselves to endure the day's responsibilities by evaluating together your priorities.

    c. Decide what is most important and don't allow unimportant things to dissipate your energy.
    d. Pray for God's wisdom to discern priorities and the discipline to follow them.

REFLECT: endurance

• • •

READ: 1 Corinthians 13:4-5       Seventeenth Day

RESPOND:
1. Encourage your partner by expressing appreciation for one of these strengths in *his* or *her* life:

    —patience       —kindness       —not jealous
    —never boastful    —never arrogant    —unselfishness
    —doesn't demand his or her own way    —not easily
                                     provoked

2. Select a quality from the above list in which *you* need improvement.
3. Share with your partner your evaluation. Pray for each other's improvement in love toward one another.

REFLECT: love

• • •

READ: Philippians 4:11-12       Eighteenth Day

RESPOND:
1. Remind each other today of something for which we should be content.
   Examples: shelter, health, food, or freedom to witness
2. What luxury can we live without, and in its place invest in something for spiritual enrichment?
3. Plan for specific times when you can express gratefulness rather than frustration.

REFLECT: contentment

• • •

READ:  James 5:7-8, 10                    Nineteenth Day

RESPOND:
1. Tell your partner when you feel he or she is most impatient.
2. What could you suggest to help him/her handle this frustration, in view of the Lord's coming?
3. Encourage your partner to remind you of His coming, the next time he or she sees any evidence of impatience.
4. Pray for each other to practice godly patience.

REFLECT:  patience

• • •

READ:  John 15:11                    Twentieth Day

RESPOND:
1. Tell your partner when you feel *he* or *she* is experiencing his or her greatest joy.
2. Express a time when *you* experience joy.
3. Plan so that your partner can experience this fullness of joy today or this week.

REFLECT:  joy

• • •

READ:  Luke 4:22;                    Twenty-first Day
          Ecclesiastes 10—12

RESPOND:
1. Ask your partner what he or she would appreciate most in terms of gracious comments when you are together in public.
2. When was the last time you complimented your partner in the presence of someone else?
3. Pray and ask God to give you opportunity for gracious

words (rather than cutting ones) for your partner in public.

REFLECT: graciousness

•  •  •

READ: Matthew 20:20-28          Twenty-second Day

RESPOND:
1. Discuss ways to show humble service.
2. Name one irritating situation of someone squeezing ahead to "be first" (restaurant line, traffic, supermarket).
3. Express appreciation to your partner for one way he or she is in an unnoticed position or second place rather than being first.
4. Thank God for your partner's willingness to serve in menial tasks.
5. Ask God to help you today to allow others to go first when tempted to have a "me-first" attitude.

REFLECT: humble service.

•  •  •

READ: John 14:26-27 and          Twenty-third Day
          Matthew 5:9 (opt. 2 Peter 3:14, LB)

RESPOND:
1. Pray for sensitivity to be a peacemaker.
2. Pray for a specific time today when you can exhibit God's peace to someone else. Allow moments of quietness and listening to God in your quiet time so the Holy Spirit can teach this to you.

REFLECT: peace

•  •  •

READ: Romans 12:15          Twenty-fourth Day

RESPOND:
Ask your partner these questions:
1. When have I rejoiced with you in the last few weeks?
2. When have I wept with you in the last few weeks?
3. When do you *wish* I would rejoice with you?
4. When do you *wish* I would hurt with you?

REFLECT: empathy

• • •

READ: Psalm 119:164                Twenty-fifth Day
(memorize verse)

RESPOND:
1. Today, consciously think about praising God.
   Perhaps noting these seven times will help:
   when waking
   breakfast
   mid-morning
   lunchtime
   mid-afternoon
   dinnertime
   bedtime
2. Praise Him for what He gives, for what He permits, and for what He withholds.

REFLECT: continual praise

• • •

READ: Genesis 2:2, Mark 6:31        Twenty-sixth Day

RESPOND:
1. Each partner should express several activities which give her/him emotional refreshment.
2. Plan for a time during the next two weeks (mark it on your calendar) when you can "come apart and rest" individually and as a twosome.

REFLECT: rest and refreshment

• • •

READ: 1 Thessalonians 2:7          Twenty-seventh Day

RESPOND:
1. Name a specific instance where you appreciate the gentleness of your partner.
2. Name a specific instance in your own life when you were not gentle.
3. Pray, asking the Lord to help you with this quality.

REFLECT: gentleness

• • •

READ: Philippians 2:3-4          Twenty-eighth Day

RESPOND:
1. Tell your partner of a recent act of unselfishness he or she did which you appreciate.
2. Thank him or her for the unselfishness you appreciate in his or her life.
3. Pray and thank God for your partner's act of unselfishness.

REFLECT: unselfishness

• • •

READ: Romans 12:10          Twenty-ninth Day

RESPOND:
1. Recall one time when you have been honored by your partner. Thank each other for this.
2. How can you and your partner honor someone outside your own relationship? Examples:
   a. Entertain a fellow Christian (time and attention, perhaps a meal).

b. Write an expression of appreciation or encouragement to one who serves unnoticed.
c. Purchase a small gift to honor someone who is seldom
recognized for his contribution to others.
3. Plan a specific time when you can honor someone in this
way.

REFLECT: honor

• • •

READ: Galatians 6:2,              Thirtieth Day
Matthew 11:28-29

RESPOND:
1. Tell your partner what burden you would like to share
with him or her. In what areas would you most appreciate your partner's support?
2. Thank God for His promise of rest. Ask God to help you
bear the burden He desires for you while gaining the
insights He wants to give you.

REFLECT: sharing burdens

• • •

READ: Hebrews 10:24           Thirty-first Day

RESPOND:
1. Think back on this month's activities. Did you meet
your goal of the first day?
2. Share with your partner specific examples of when you
have been stimulated to love and good deeds.
3. Ask God to increase your awareness of your partner's
needs so that you can better reflect God's qualities.

REFLECT: evaluation

# Talks with the Lord

## 8

The verse in this section could never win a poetry contest—it is not meant to compete. It is included in this book because I want to share with you some of my own thoughts and hurts. All of them are part of my own "Listening to God" notebook.

## Time for God on a Christian Campus?

A new semester has begun.
   The campus is teeming with life . . .
      happy, yet confused faces—
      "This class is closed—"
      "To find employment, fill out these forms. . . ."
      "Class 304 has been changed to room 102. . . ."
      "That textbook isn't in yet . . . try again tomorrow."
      "If you hurry, you can still make lunch. . . ."
   When, Lord, will I have time to listen to You?
         *"When you are willing to take the time."*


Students are friendly, but frustrated,
   Lines are endless
      to the faculty advisor,
      to the registrar,
      to the cafeteria,
      to the financial aid office,
      to the business office,
      to the bookstore

            *"But I see no line to the prayer
               chapel—does no one long to
               be with Me?"*

· · ·

OK, Lord, I'm finally on my way to a special place
   to spend some time with You . . .
   but on the way,
      I should really stop at the bookstore and pick up that
         syllabus!
      My stomach is so empty—a snack at the coffee shop will
         take just a minute.
      And oh, my mailbox . . . I can't forget that—it's right on
         the way!
      Well, there's Jan—I really shouldn't ignore her—
      Just one more stop, Lord,

I do need to get that book at the library
before anyone else does.
. . . Ooops, looks like my time with You will have to
wait, Lord,
I'm sorry, I'll try and make it tomorrow.
*"Will I merely be an acquaintance*
*when you come to live in your*
*heavenly home?"*

## Walk in My Shoes, Lord

Walk in my shoes today, Lord,
    reveal Yourself through me . . .
Show others that it is really You
    Who lives in this earthly frame.

        Smile through my eyes, Lord;
            lift someone's spirits today . . .
        Reveal Your winsomeness, Holy Spirit,
            in my temporary shell of flesh and bone.

Live through my actions, Lord,
    and while You have taken residence inside me,
Provide the experiences that result from prayer closet promises,
    so that my spiritual fiber will stretch
        to full stature—
    and by living in me,
    You can reveal Your glory.

## 20th-Century Hideaway

Lord, You have placed me here
    in the 20th century,
  a world of
    screaming jets,
    instant media,
    rattling computers,
  a world sometimes hard to understand.

Sometimes I ache, just to be out of it,
    away from the
    freeway rat race,
    polluted air,
    bombardment of sound.

But through it all,
    You draw me to Yourself—
      to the secret,
        quiet place of strength,
    where You shut out the noise,
        chaos, and
        confusion . . .
      to teach me how
      to reflect the gentle Jesus
    here in this 20th century.

## Pharisaism

Oh, Lord, how can it be
  that even in Christian circles
  where we all know You (or are supposed to!),
    living a double standard seems so common . . .
      I flinch at the pulling of strings,
        the politics for prestige,
        the walking on people to get ahead,
        the pious innuendos for putting others down
          so we can look better—

It's so difficult for me to understand
  how we can be such Pharisees
    —if we really *learn to know You better day by day,*
    —if we really *listen* to what You want for us,
    —if we *desire* to develop a sensitiveness to our
      brothers in Your body,
    —if we really *want* to be like You!

The burden of this really weighs me down, Lord,
The pact I once made with You to not defend myself
    almost blows wide open—
  when tolerant tongues tingle with self-righteous twitter . . .
  when struggle for status strangles Your beauty in
    personalities . . .
  when apple-polishing takes precedence over servant
    attitude . . .
  when closet-praying is so minimal
    and judging others is so maximal . . .
  when caring is obviously at the
      bottom
      of
      the
      list.

Dear Lord, don't let condescending eyes,
   and jealous attitudes
      tempt me to break my covenant with You.
I will *not* retaliate.
I will *not* strike back,
   and give the enemy the satisfaction
   that I have lost my cool.
And when I don't understand,
   when disappointment floods me,
   when transparency in people—even Your children,
      seems to disappear,
   Give me the courage to stand alone
    and know that it's worth it all
      to do my very best
      to act like You did when You were here on earth.

## Problems

The problem facing me seems so huge now
  in my own small, finite self,
But looking at it from Your eyes,
  how tiny in the span of eternity!

It's so easy to build up momentous decisions . . .
  in my own insignificance.
Yet, in Your perspective
  they are like one of the numberless sands
    on the seashore.

In my one little corner,
I can raise a cloud of dust
  over what seems to be
  a gigantic issue—
How much better to just listen to You!

Lord, help me to daily
  see the problems,
    attitudes,
    reactions,
  through Your understanding of the
    scope of eternity.
Perhaps, then, my huge problems
  will crumble into unimportant nothings
  and I can be at peace with the world.

## Pride

Who am I, that I should be known
   in this century?
   on this earth,
   in this galaxy?

For I am important to You
   before You created the earth,
   before You created the galaxies,
   forever and always!

For I belong to You
   to be known by You,
   to be loved by You,
   to be used by You.

So keep me from the pride of self-sufficiency;
   Use me as Your servant
     to listen to others,
     to care for others,
     to pray for others,
      in this century,
      on this earth
      in my corner
       *now.*

## Forgiveness

Lord, don't let my life sit like a rusted pipe,
   once flowing with Your activity—
   now closed with the corrosion
      of hurt,
         unforgiveness,
         judging,
         criticism,
         dogmatism.

Help me realize, Lord, that
   Your sweet waters flow through me
  when my mind is open,
     my eyes are on You—not others,
  when I'm not judgmental,
    not dogmatic,
    not attention-seeking
      or critical,

  but forgiving, merciful, gentle.
Then our minds, Yours and mine,
  mingle on the same wave length—
Then Your quiet joy can flow through me to others
  and You can use me again to minister.

## Pain

Lord, thank You for helping me to realize
 that when You entrust us with pain,
  physical or otherwise,
 that genuine pain is not to be paraded before others
   for all to see . . .
  not to be attention-seeking,
   so others can sigh with empathy.

You allow us pain for growth, maturity in You,
 to better understand Your suffering,
 we are given just a measure—
  and then we love You more!

Pain, then, is something to be shared with You,
 not to be displayed in a window glass
  for the world to inspect.
It is something precious which You entrust to those
 to be used as a magnet
 to draw us nearer Your heart,
  so that in daily living our radiance is
   sweeter,
   softer,
   more sensitive.
 And that in our relating to others, we can
   encourage,
   affirm,
   uplift
   children of Yours in their pilgrimage with You.

Thank you for teaching me, Lord,
 that although warm and safe, human comfort
  is but temporary,
   only for a time.

And that in my secret closet, as I bring this wound to You,
   as Your firm arms enfold me, hold and comfort me,
   as You inoculate me with Your whispers of gentle caring,
The pain You have allowed diminishes under Your touch.

Thank You for this lesson, then.

For because of it—you are ever nearer than before.

## The Blessing of Small, Quiet Corners

Why is it, Lord, that so many of us seek the route of the large,
      the popular,
      the prominent,
      the renowned?
      How this must grieve You.

    for You have said Yourself,
       and have set the example,
       that to be a leader
         we must serve.

  Who of us is really willing to serve You
     in an unnoticed community,
       an unimportant church,
       an unesteemed group,
       a small place?
         Then having grown through
         the hard knocks,
           is seasoned to lead!
  Where are we, Lord?

So many of us are willing, yes, anxious
  to do those things we are sure will be observed by men.
But who of us is willing to bend low to "wash the disciples'
     feet"?
Impress on us Your attitudes,
  so that in the shadows we can fulfill those menial tasks,
    so unworthy in the sight of man—
    but worth everything to You.

  Thank You, Lord, for this lesson . . .
    that the pleasing of fickle men
    makes no impression on You whatever,
     but

that obedience to You in those small, quiet corners
pleases You the most . . .

that the true test of Your child
   is not how well we perform in man's eyes,
   but how we obey You in the lowly servant tasks
      You set before us to do.

## Transparentness

Lord, create in me a lucidness in my earthly walk,
    a sincere childlikeness,
    a clear winsomeness,
    a willing openness,
  so others can look right through me
      and see You.
First, stand in the very center of me,
    so that Your light
    inspects every crevice,
    revealing to all who may care to look
  that you are my daily searchlight.

Then, Lord, pull up the blinds of my life,
    so it is clear as glass,
    transparent, for others to look through—
      and see You.

Thank You, for accompanying me, Lord
    through this risk of being vulnerable.
Perhaps now, others might be willing
    to drop their masks,
    so You can truly be seen
      through them too.

## Preferences

Let books be written,
Let conferences be conducted,
Let meetings be convened,
    But my Saviour is here with me
        and I listen.
    He wants me here with Him.

Let awards be given,
Let honors be bestowed,
Let wealth be earned,
    But my Saviour is here with me
        and I listen.
    He wants me here with Him.

Let the media spout forth its knowledge,
Let the world pass by,
Let this planet perish if it will,
    But my Saviour is here with me
        and I listen.
    He wants me here with Him.

> *"Dear child,*
>     *your presence*
>         *is more precious*
>         *than any project you do for Me—*
>     *I delight to have you*
>         *by My side."*

## The Crossing

Lord, as we crossed from the old year to the new
   You prepared to call our daddy Home,
      as his life hung in the balance.
We were so sure he would stay with us—
   but You had other plans.

Just as You told the Israelites that You would protect them
   as they crossed the Jordan River,
You stood in the middle of our crisis,
   and helped us cross into the New Year.
You strengthened us for Daddy's crossing,
   as well as our own.

And just as You commanded
   that a monument be made from stones of that river,
Today I want to honor my father in words to You, Lord,
   that would be a verbal memorial to him.

Thank you, Lord, for a dad who instilled in me
     the joys of great music,
     the glories of Your sunsets,
     the delights of snow in winter
       and growing things in summer . . .
   for a dad who struggled during Depression years
     to feed and clothe us,
   for a dad who built for us a yard of happy memories,
     full of flowers, trees, and playhouse,
     while outside an insecure world fought a war.

Most of all, Lord,
   thank You for the heritage he gave us
     to love You, to trust You,
     to prepare for heaven and Your Presence,

for as long as I live,
    this heritage will linger on
    through me to the lives of others.

Now his work has been completed,
    and he has crossed
        from our time-bound planet
        to Your everlasting arms.

*—in memory of my father,*
*Ralph T. Neuenschwander*
*January 10, 1978*

## Arrival in Heaven

Oh Lord, what must it be like
    to enter Your presence?
This morning as the clouds glowed pink and gold
    at the first hint of sunrise—
It was as if the heavens were smiling in salute
    to one of its newest arrivals—
Yesterday we lost a dear friend from our presence,
    but it was her welcome into Yours.

What's it like, those first moments with You . . .
    and with Your other children from so many centuries back,
    living now in Your home?
It's difficult for us, trapped by time,
    to see Your perspective of eternity.
How wonderful that our friend now has that perspective too.

Lord, another of my friends is very near Your door . . .
    She is young, with husband and family.
She knows she is on the threshold
    of entering Your presence.
Her family knows. Her friends know.
She belongs to You, Lord. Shouldn't that be a comfort?
    Then why are we so careful not to mention it?

Why can't we freely talk about our entrance into heaven?
    Our joyful reunion with You?
Is it our fear of the unknown?
    Our sympathy for those left behind?
    Death to us, is precious to You.
While we try to pretend it won't happen,
    or wish we could somehow delay it,
    You are there, joyfully watching for us to come,
        waiting for our arrival.

Lord, give us Your perspective to accept with joy
   the fact that You created us to be here
      for only a few moments,
      in the span of eternity with You!

*—in memory of*
*Lillian Braun*

## Acceptance of Death

Lord, I feel like a pile of yarn,
   all tangled up.
Death looked me in the face today
   and I hurt inside.
Two lovely ladies, both dear friends,
   will soon lift up their eyes to look at You.
They know it and so do I.

Death had always come to someone older,
   parent or relative,
Now it sits close beside me,
   by friends near my age
   who have shared my hopes,
     my hurts,
     my happiness.

Shouldn't I be joyful—glad they'll be with You?
Yet a whole new arena of feelings
   surrounds me.
   Old feelings, but in a foreign situation—
     uselessness,
      frustration,
       confusion,
   my total inability to help anyone!

I don't ask why, Lord, I do accept Your will,
But as I try and unscramble my feelings,
   sort through my thoughts,
The knowledge is comforting
   that even though my friends will leave me,
You will take them home to be more complete
   than they are now.
And You are in control of this situation.

## This Close to Heaven

For two and a half hours we talked, Lord,
   your special child and I,
About what heaven will be like
   when You take her home
     any time now.
       It was so beautiful, so open,
         this time together.
       We shared so many things,
         not just past, but future.

She'll be with You, Lord,
   face-to-face.
She'll know the joy
   of Your physical presence,
   of never leaving You.

       I told her I was envious
         of her homegoing,
       Because she'll leave this world,
         she'll see the beauties of heaven.

We talked of her baby son
   who died at three weeks.
She said she would know him.
She glowed when she said that.

       I asked her to tell the Lord,
         "Please come soon."
       But then, I guess He's tarrying,
         for those who've never heard,
       And they should have a chance, too!

Her body is changing, Lord,
   from a disease so little known,

But her eyes were radiant
   as she talked of leaving earth
   and going to live with You.

     Lord, she's such a special friend,
       we've shared for many years,
     But to You she's so select,
       because You've chosen her
       to take that special journey.

These two and a half hours, Lord,
   were precious in my life,
For they were spent with someone
   who will soon be with You . . .
And for now, that's as close to heaven
   as I can come.

*—in honor of Inez Gooden*

## Strangers in Heaven?

Oh, Lord, will we be strangers in heaven?
  Will introductions need to be made?
  Because I didn't have time for You here on earth?
The very thought drives me to Your side!

When I measure my scant years spent on this planet,
  in relation to the scope of time
  (will the word "time" even exist in eternity?),
I tremble to reflect on how little I really know You,
And yet, how intimate our everlasting union will be!

If, in our new bodies, memories will be a part,
Then thoughts like these will surely haunt me—
  How could I have been so engrossed with pint-sized
      problems,
    so swayed by man-made media,
    so impressed with people-praise
  to have let such priceless get-acquainted times
    with You slip by?

Thank You for teaching me
  that when it seems the most impossible to meet with You,
it is during *these* encounters when the reward of Your presence
    is the most precious . . .
  that Your perspective of timelessness
    lingers with me throughout the day
    and we are strangers no longer.

1 John 2:28

## Heaven is Waiting

Heaven, My child, will be precious,
for you will be by My side,
I no longer will have to wait for you to come and talk with Me,
for you will always be near Me.             Ps. 116:15

Heaven, My child, will be glorious,
for you I left it and came to your world;
For you, I died so I could have you
with Me forever.                    John 3:16

Heaven, My child, will be eternal,
for you I have a place
Especially prepared when you arrive
and I will come personally for you
to live here with Me always.            John 14:2

Heaven, My child, will be joyous,
for you, there will be no more sorrow;
I will wipe away every tear from your eyes
and take away your night.
Here you will be happy and complete.     Rev. 7:17; 22:5

Heaven, My child, will be rewarding,
for crowns will be in abundance.
And for you there will be one special
because you are eagerly watching for my return. 2 Tim. 4:8

So don't give up, My child,
For heaven is here waiting;
Though your outer body is aging,
Renew your inner strength daily,
by getting to know Me
and be like Me.                 2 Cor. 4:14-18

For heaven, My child, is your inheritance.       1 Peter 1:4

## Healing

What a thrilling thought—
    every sunrise, every sunset
    brings me closer to the heaven
  I often think of,
      dream about,
      anticipate!

The loss of our friends brings You and heaven
  so much nearer,
    that we can almost conceive
      of happy welcomings in Your midst,
    while we remain on this sick earth.
The very thoughts of You and heaven
  bring warmth to our icy loneliness.

Thank You for these gems of comfort,
  and for planting in the mind of man
    an imagination,
  so that in his hours of grief
  he can visualize what heaven must be like with You.
And that, in these ponderings,
  the gaping cavities of our souls
  can begin to knit together once again—
    and the healing process begins.

## To Become Like You, Lord

Oh, to become like You, Lord,
   I've asked this often . . .
   I've yearned and strained and longed
      to try and copy You.
But this is not Your way
     to fashion Your child
     into Your likeness.

Only when You allow a trial
   to come and stand before me,
   to question and defy me,
Only then can I make the choice
     to accept or reject it
     as a tool to refine me
   to a better likeness of You.

When bitter words assault me,
When I long to jump to my defense,
When my pride falls and crashes
   into a million pieces—
This is the teachable moment,
     the golden opportunity,
    to allow You to strengthen my spiritual fiber
     so my attitudes become like Yours.

You accepted pain willingly,
     ungrudgingly,
     nonvindictively.
You had gone before me to experience all
    that I am to feel,
   so that I could follow
   in Your footsteps
   to become like You.

There is only one difference—
You hold my hand through my hurt,
While You went through Yours alone.

## Having Been with You

To know when to confront
    when confronting is needed,
  when to affirm
    when affirmation is lacking,
  when to care
    when caring is deficient . . .
      this special discernment is given
      after having been with You.

Lord, my deepest desire and highest goal,
  is to know Your mind,
    how You would live each day
      in my century,
      in my culture,
      in my shoes.

But to know it—I need to get acquainted with You,
  spend time with You,
  walk with You,
    every day!
  Not *If* I feel like it . . .
    *If* my schedule isn't too full . . .
    *If* I can get up on time . . .
    *If* it's convenient for me . . .
      etc., etc., etc.,
  but daily, habitually, regardless!
    —in the dark hours before sunrise, if need be.

For it is here in this discipline,
  before the blotter of my mind becomes splattered
    with input from others,
    that Your thoughts become my thoughts,
      Your insights become my insights,

Your actions become my actions,
and I am saturated with Your Spirit,

having been with You.

## Listening at Your Feet

In this century of maddening pace,
    where technology turns the realms of the impossible to
       reality,
    where science toys in areas before unknown—
       and acts like a god in life-death situations,
I shiver at the mind of man and his imagination—

      Without You, man is nothing.
      Without listening to You, he stumbles blindly along,
        making foolish decisions.
      And yet, one person, when listening to You,
        can reach into the depths of lonely lives,
          into the spirits of the broken.
      One listening heart, in keenest discernment,
        can cope with the moments of each day,
        *because he has heard Your voice.*

If I want to hear You, Lord
    I know I must turn my back on the pandemonium of my
       century—
      —on the inventions of science
      —on the thrills of new knowledge
      —on the worship of status, education, fashion, and
       dollars,
      —on even the newness of "innovations" within Christian
       circles, caught in the rhythmical rut of my culture . . .
    for I know You will never shout above this 20th-century
       clatter.
      You only wait for me
    to close my ears to it—
      so I may sit at Your feet
        and listen.